P9-DFN-403

The Grace of Silence

The Grace of Silence

Michele Norris

PANTHEON BOOKS, NEW YORK

Grateful acknowledgment is made to the Birmingham Public Library for permission to reprint an August 6, 1942, letter from Eugene "Bull" Connor to Franklin Roosevelt (Birmingham, Alabama Law Department Legal Files, Birmingham, Alabama Public Library Archives). Reprinted by permission of the Birmingham Public Library.

Library of Congress Cataloging-in-Publication Data
Norris, Michele.
The grace of silence / Michele Norris.
p. cm.
Includes bibliographical references.
ISBN 978-0-307-37876-7
1. Norris, Michele. 2. Norris, Michele—Family. 3. African American journalists—Biography. 4. African American women—Biography. 5. United States—Race relations.
I. Title.
PN4874.N64A3 2010 070.92—dc22 [B] 2010019285

www.pantheonbooks.com

Printed in the United States of America
First Edition
2 4 6 8 9 7 5 3 1

For my parents, Belvin & Betty,
You gave me wings

It is a unique art and special skill, this business of being a Negro in America.

—WILLIAM H. HASTIE
Lawyer, Judge, Civil Rights Advocate,
Civilian Aide to the Secretary of War

CONTENTS

INTRODUCTION

I BEGAN THIS PROJECT in 2009 because I became convinced that an unprecedented, hidden, and robust conversation about race was taking place across the country in the wake of Barack Obama's historic presidential campaign and his ascension to office. Americans seemed to be spending more time talking about race, but even so, I had the feeling that something was always left unsaid. Filters would automatically engage, preventing us from saying things that might cause us embarrassment or get us into trouble or, even worse, reveal us for who we really are. We weren't so much talking about race as talking around it.

In my work at National Public Radio, I tried to dig deep into race in America in a multipart NPR series of no-holds-barred conversations with a diverse group of voters in York, Pennsylvania. Over the course of three visits we spent more than fifteen hours with fifteen Americans: whites, blacks, Latinos, and South Asians. We were surprised by their enthusiasm for the project. We eased the conversation with good meals. (Amazing how carbohydrates can lubricate a conversation.) And we asked simple and direct questions. What are the occasions, if any, when you become aware of your race? Do white Americans underestimate discrimination? Do black people make too much of it? How would the country be different if led by a black man?

There was candor, discomfort, and a certain amount of conflict among those gathered in the room. They rolled their eyes and crossed their arms and conveyed their unease in myriad ways. They did so many of the things that people do before unease turns to exasperation and the possibility of conversation vanishes. But they didn't back down, even when things got dicey. All stayed and listened, even as each revealed fears, biases, hopes, and insecurities—all those things so often left unsaid when people try to talk about race. In the end, we were confident we had pushed past a barrier to frankness and had probed the consequence of silence on matters of race.

What happened in York is by no means unique. It is happening right now in beauty parlors and truck stops, in college dormitories and courthouses, in office parks, at construction sites, and at dinner tables, where parents are often confronted by children with more tolerant views on race. The conversation is flowing through bodegas and along interstate highways and rural roads. It is filling computer screens and creeping into country clubs.

Yet for the most part, it remains segregated. Blacks and other people of color often seem to talk about race more openly, while many whites appear to yearn for a postracial world where such discussions are unnecessary. People may be talking about race more, but they're not necessarily talking to one another. My intention was to eavesdrop on their conversations and write a book that might enrich our collective dialogue on the thorny subject.

Well, the truth can set you free, but it can also be profoundly disconcerting. I realized that pretty quickly when I began listening carefully to conversations in my own family. I had hoped that other people would speak candidly about race for my book, but I soon came to understand that my reporting had to begin with me. The discussion about race within my own family was not completely honest.

My racial identity has largely been forged by the sum of experiences in my lifetime, and my most formative memories flow through my parents' lives—from their struggles and tribulations, their triumphs and celebrations, their dignity found through a hard day's work, the devotion of our worship, the places we lived, and, above all, the constant expectation captured by one word: *rise.* Rise and shine. Rise to the occasion. Rise above it all. No matter what, move forward, never backward, always onward and upward. And if you ever feel like you're at the end of your rope, tie a knot and hold on until you can start climbing again.

For all of our lives, we were told, "Keep your eye on the prize." Stay strong. Keep committed. Focus on the fight for justice and equality. Set your sights on excellence and opportunity. Don't let up. Don't look back. Don't slow down. Ignore the slights and the slurs—and the laws—that try to keep you from achieving your goals. Always keep the prize in mind. See it. Smell it. Feel it. Our parents armed us with what they thought we needed: strength, courage, and a touch of indignation. But just a touch.

I was shaped by the advice and admonitions that rained down on me. I've always known that. What I did not know until I began this project is that I was also shaped by the weight of my parents' silence. I originally wanted to write about how "other people" talked about race, but that presumption was swiftly disabused when I learned about secrets in my own family that had purposely been kept from me.

Among those secrets was this: as a young man, my father had been shot by a white policeman. He never spoke about the incident after leaving Alabama and moving north. He never told even my mother. He took the story to his grave. But she, too, was hiding something. My mother never talked about the time her mother spent working as a traveling Aunt Jemima, swooping through small midwestern towns in a hoop skirt and head scarf to perform pancake-making demonstrations for farm women. The memory had caused her shame, so she'd locked it away. These revelations suggest to me that in certain ways I've never had a full understanding of my parents or of the formation of my own racial identity.

How many of us know the whole truth about our families? For most of my adult life, I thought I did, but my confidence has been shaken. One of the unforeseen consequences of the rise of Barack Obama has been a grudging willingness to shed painful memories. The rise of a black man to the nation's highest office has lowered the barrier for painful conversations among Americans of all colors, especially those who lived through the trials and tumult of forced segregation.

Every household is different; in my childhood home, the window to that painful past was never widely opened. Instead, stories were meted out judiciously, in morsels and tidbits. Occasionally, there would be a tale of a hardscrabble life or some unguarded talk. A visiting relative—fueled by that third glass of Pink Champale—would steer the conversation toward a place called melancholy and then a bit yonder, to the rough intersection where disappointment meets rage. But it would never last long. The story would always come to an abrupt end. My mother would shoot one of her "don't go there" looks, and the discussion would snap back to the here and now. Even so, something in that relative's face—a sudden gloss in the eyes, a catch in the throat—suggested a mind still wandering through some distant, aching memory.

Our parents felt we needed to know only so much. No time for tears. No yearning for sympathy. You see, you can't keep your eye on the prize if your sight is clouded by tears. How can you soar if you're freighted down by the anger of your ancestors?

The Grace of Silence

I

Daddy

MY FATHER WAS ONE OF those people who are most comfortable at the fringes, away from the action center stage. He did not need or crave attention. Instead, he was driven by the need to reassure others that everything was going to be all right. Belvin Norris Jr. was a fixer. An eternal optimist to the core. You could see it in his smile. As a grown man he still grinned like a schoolboy, and you could not help but grin along with him. His vibe was contagious. Kindness is usually seen as altruistic. But it can also be an act of desperation, satisfying a deep-seated need to avoid the mind's darker places. Benevolence, for some, is a survival tactic.

Even in his last hours my father practiced benevolence, always looking out for everybody else. Moments after the doctor delivered devastating news about his health, my father, still smiling, pointed to an infected cut on my left hand. It was his way of prodding the emergency room physician to turn his attention to me. The victim opting to be the benefactor.

Dad took ill in June 1988, while visiting his brother Simpson in Fort Wayne, Indiana. The minute he called me I knew something awful had happened. His voice was graveled, his words rubbery. He couldn't put a sentence together, and the failed effort only added to his frustration. He had lost control of his speech, but he managed to hold on to his sunny disposition. Although his words were incomprehensible, I sensed a false cheer, with each attempt at speech ending on an elevated note—the kind of verbal leap parents of very young children use to mask irritation or fear.

I was working as a newspaper reporter in Chicago at the time. Dad had stopped by to visit me on his way to Uncle Simpson's house. We had spent a few days going to baseball games and trying to get my kitchen in order. He was relieved to see that I'd finally learned to enjoy spending time at the stove. I showed off for him with jambalaya and pineapple upside-down cake. It worked. He set small talk aside, went back for seconds, and still had room for a huge piece of cake. When he was finished he dabbed his mouth and said, "Maybe now you'll find someone who will put up with you."

To another person, this might have sounded like a dig, but I knew what he meant. I could use my kitchen skills to cook at home and save money and to help "close the deal" when I found the right man. I was twenty-six and living on my own in Chicago. No husband. No roommate. Just me in a second-story duplex apartment with high ceilings, a large kitchen, and actual furniture. For years my father had visited me at various apartments where the most comfortable chair had been either a wooden crate or something recovered from the curb on trash day. He never let me forget an embarrassing episode when I was living in southern California. A neighbor stopped by my Manhattan Beach apartment to borrow a coffee filter one Saturday morning. She couldn't stop staring at the wingback armchair in which my father sat reading the *Los Angeles Times.* "You know, Michele," she said, "that looks like the chair I threw out for bulk trash pickup a few weeks ago."

My neighbor left with her borrowed coffee filter and a piece of my dignity. Lucky for me, my father had a sense of humor and a strong commitment to thrift. He always believed that the prettiest car on the road was the one that was paid in full, and in his book the most attractive chair in my cramped living room that day was the one that had arrived without a price tag. We had a good laugh, and when he left, he snuck an envelope into my jewelry box with "sofa fund" written on the outside.

My father preached that he would always help me as long as I helped myself by working hard and spending smart. I was better at the former than the latter. When he visited me in Chicago in June 1988, he saw that I had earned high marks on both fronts. He appeared healthy during that visit. A week later, when I got the call from Indiana, it seemed I was talking to a man I didn't know. As soon as I put the phone down, I started packing a bag. I had to get to Fort Wayne fast. By the time I arrived, Dad had already checked into the hospital. The doctors there didn't know exactly what was wrong, but they knew that something was very wrong and that most likely it had to do with his brain or his central nervous system. The doctors spoke among themselves about anaplastic astrocytomas and radiation therapy. It was a code that could mean only one thing: cancer.

Even in the most terrifying moments at a sterile hospital, there is some comfort in knowing that a world you recognize is just outside and beyond the parking garage. You can fixate on a familiar image as a doctor shaves years off your life with each sentence. He can talk all he wants about therapies and operations, but you're thinking of the parking lot where you taught your daughter to drive, or the gas station that uses red reflective press-on letters to spell out a different Bible verse each week, like "The fear of the Lord is the beginning of wisdom." While the doctor yammers on, you're thinking of the grizzled gas station attendant who climbs the ladder to change the sign, and wondering what pearl of wisdom he might offer in light of the news you just got.

In Fort Wayne, in a large hospital in an unfamiliar city, we were confronting an unknown illness that had swiftly robbed my father of his ability to carry out the most basic functions. We were looking at complicated surgery and, at best, a long and complex recovery, so the doctors suggested that we quickly move Dad back to Minnesota, where he could be treated closer to home.

We wanted to get Dad on the first flight to the Twin Cities, but his gait was unsteady and he seemed increasingly disoriented. He clutched my arm as we walked through the airport; he kept shooting me tight little smiles: reassurance. I wasn't buying it. By now his speech was so slurred that only I could understand him, and so labored that he wasn't able even to whisper. It took him so much effort and focus to spit out a sound that it was slightly explosive when it arrived, like a sputtering engine in a hushed area.

At the airport we sat across from two stout middle-aged blond women with wet-set curls and matching pink satin jackets. They must have been on their way to a convention or a sorority gathering; they were electric with excitement and frosted up like high-calorie confections, constantly rifling through their pocketbooks for mirrored compacts, then checking their makeup or blotting their lipstick. I remember them so well because they were sitting next to a large Amish or Mennonite family.

The men had long beards and wore suspenders. The women had long braids and long dresses, and their heads were covered by little white hats that looked like fancy French fry baskets. They seemed uncomfortable with the constant chatter of the satin dolls. They, too, noticed the women's prying eyes and "get a load of this" gestures, though the taciturn demeanor of the Amish rendered them perhaps slightly less interesting specimens than Dad and me.

When my dad tried to lean toward me to ask a question, his words sputtered forth like bricks tumbling from a shelf. The satin dolls found it hard to mind their own business. They stared and pointed every time Dad attempted to speak. They didn't try to hide their disparagement, one of them harrumphing loud enough for anyone to hear, "Goodness sakes, it's not even noon yet!"

After spending a lifetime trying to be a model minority—one of the few black men in his neighborhood, at his workplace, or on his daughters' school committees—my father now sat facing the condemnation of the two blond scolds. They had apparently concluded that he was an early morning lush instead of a gray-haired man fighting a losing battle with a devastating disease.

Here is the conundrum of racism. You know it's there, but you can't prove, beyond a reasonable doubt, how it colors a particular situation. Those pink satin ladies were strangers to me, so I have no idea if they would have been as quick to judge a gray-haired white man with impaired speech. However, I do know this: the fact that they were white women added mightily to my father's humiliation. I knew my father felt the sting of their judgment. I knew it because he kept pushing up his cardigan sleeve and futzing with his wrist, as if he'd left home without his Timex. But it was not the wrist on which he wore his windup watch. It was the wrist where the plastic bracelet had been affixed at the hospital. His awkward gestures were a silent plea to the satin dolls to notice the hospital bracelet. My heart breaks every time I think of the look on his face that day.

The jut of his chin showed indignation, but the sag of his shoulders and the crease in his brow conveyed something different. Something hovering between anger and shame. There was also, however, a hint of grace. I see that now that I have come to understand my father better, as a man who was always in tight control of his emotions. I believe now that he was trying not just to salvage his dignity but also to absolve the two women from dishonor. A less controlled, more impulsive man might have responded by giving those women the finger to shut them up. My father drew strength from reaching past anger.

The aphorism "Kill them with kindness" might have been penned with a man like Belvin Norris Jr. in mind. By fiddling with his wrist he was saying, "If only they knew," rather than "Shame on you."

Dad boarded the plane early because the flight crew knew he would need extra time to settle into his seat and because they wanted to check his medical release from the hospital. He was flying alone that morning. I planned to drive his Oldsmobile back to Minneapolis and meet him there the next morning, a decision I have spent a lifetime regretting. Before walking down the jetway, he motioned for the nurse and the flight crew to wait a second. He leaned toward me as if he wanted to tell me something, but he couldn't get words out. He kept looking over his shoulder, aware of the flight crew watching and waiting, and perhaps wondering whether the satin dolls were also taking it all in. He kissed me on the cheek, a loving but clumsy gesture. His balance was off, so it was almost as if we were bumping heads. I didn't mind, and I certainly didn't care who was watching as we locked in a long embrace. My eyes were closed, fighting back tears, so I barely noticed when the flight attendant crept into our circle of grief to gently remind us that they had to stay on schedule. The attendant lightly cupped my father's elbow and led him away. It is disturbing to see your parent treated like a schoolchild, yet amusing to watch a man grin like a lucky teenager when a pretty woman takes his arm.

As I walked away, the satin dolls gazed at me. They must have overheard the chat about Dad's medical release because now they wore pouty, ingratiating smiles. Lipstick contrition. I walked past them and smiled back. It hurts to recall my response; I, like my father, had reached beyond anger to offer conciliation instead. I had every right to throw my father's humiliation in their faces. Spitting at them was, of course, out of bounds, but at the very least I should have served up a scowl.

I should have made them squirm. I should have been the black girl that certain white women are conditioned to fear most.

I didn't do any of that. I am my father's daughter, and such caustic gestures weren't in my DNA. I was raised by a model minority to be a model minority, and to achieve that status, certain impulses had to be suppressed. Years later, I understand both the reason and its consequence.

I was almost out of the waiting area when I felt someone touch my shoulder. I turned, thinking it might be one of the women, intent on apologizing, but there was no nail polish on the hand touching my arm. The hand was large and calloused, marked by raised splotches resembling coffee stains. A bearded man held my forearm; he called me "ma'am," though it sounded like "Mom." "I'll watch over your pa," he said before darting back to join his family.

I wonder what my father had wanted to tell me, but couldn't, right before he'd boarded the plane. More of his classic lunchbox wisdom? "Learn all you can" or "Save your money" or "Don't eat too much late at night"? More than twenty years later, as still I mourn, I wonder if he was trying to impart some eternal verity before his final flight home to Minneapolis. This would be the last time I saw him alert. Within a day Dad slipped into a coma. Within a week a fast-growing brain tumor took his life.

2

Block Busters

BEFORE THE ALARM CLOCK GOES OFF, before the smell of coffee or bacon finds its way to your bedroom door, there's often a sound outside your window that jolts you out of slumber during winter months in Minnesota. It's the scrape of a snow shovel against wet cement. I know the sound so well. The thwack of the blade cutting through snow, the drag of metal across pavement, the thump of the payload landing somewhere on the lawn.

Thwack, swoosh, thud! Three steps in four-quarter rhythm, over and over, until the job is done. The thought sends an all-too-familiar ache through my shoulders. All the same, in my house as a child, I myself rarely awoke to the sounds of snow being shoveled. I listened to it going on outside my kitchen window while wolfing down Malt-O-Meal or scrambled eggs. You see, by the time the rest of the neighborhood began their collective assault on the snow, our walkway was already whistle clean. That was a point of pride for my father. When the Westvigs and the Murrays and the Bowmans and the Pratts ventured out of their stucco homes, they would look over and see that the sidewalk around Belvin and Betty Norris's lot was already free of snow and ice. Dad would be in the house, sipping coffee, a self-satisfied grin on his face, tiny icicles still dangling from his mustache. My parents were always house proud.

We lived on a corner lot on the South Side of Minneapolis,

which was at once a blessing and a curse. In the summer, it meant we had a larger yard to play in and nearly an extra hour of daylight. Oakland Avenue was lined with towering elms that formed a thick, protective canopy. But our intersection broke up the tree line and toward the end of day we could look to the sky from our two-story Tudor house with its curved ten-foot bay window. At sundown the glow would radiate through that window like lemonade spilling out of a pitcher. We called it the golden hour.

In winter the corner lot meant extra work. We didn't just have to clear the T-shaped stretch of sidewalk that led from our stone steps to the street. We also had the fan-shaped curve at the corner to contend with, the long stretch of cement along the side of the house, the driveway leading up to the garage, and the opening to the alley. All that, and no sons in the house. So as soon as I could walk I was given an itty-bitty shovel. First a plastic one to get the feel of the thing, but within a year or two, a junior version of an adult shovel, wood and metal. A shovel was a tool for survival in Minnesota, so you had better get the hang of it early on. Though it's not written down anywhere, there is strict shoveling etiquette in Minneapolis. No matter how much snow falls the night before, you are obliged to clear your walkway and driveway before leaving the house in the morning. No exceptions. My father went one step further and decreed that snow had to be cleared before our neighbors arose. No matter what, you had to adjust. Six inches of snow: wake up forty-five minutes early. Twelve inches of snow: better make that two hours. If it was a whopper of a storm, you'd do some shoveling before bedtime to skim the first few inches, then rise early to shovel the rest, satisfied that your work the night before had reduced the morning's accumulation.

For a man raised in the Birmingham heat, my father took to this with alacrity. He'd suit up in big black galoshes and a tight little watch cap and head outside like Teddy Roosevelt preparing to charge San Juan Hill. Everybody shoveled. Mom. Me. My two half sisters, Cindy and Marguerite. No use complaining or you'd pull double duty. This, too, was a point of pride. We were a family of hardworking folk, and my parents looked for every opportunity to trumpet the note. Belvin and Betty Norris were block busters when they purchased their stucco home near the Minnehaha Parkway in South Minneapolis. "We weren't trying to be activists," my mother said. "We just decided it was time to live someplace nice. We worked hard and we worked with white people at the post office who could live wherever they wanted. We wanted to do the same thing and we wanted to show them that we could do the same thing. We wanted to show them that we were just as good as they were."

The Twin Cities, especially Minneapolis, were known for tolerance. Even so, blacks, Latinos, American Indians, and, later, Hmong and Vietnamese refugees would cluster in a few ethnic fiefdoms. My parents wanted to be on the far South Side, where the best schools were located, and they wanted to be close to water. Finding a house wasn't going to be easy for a brown-skinned couple. Realtors would "forget" appointments or make hasty exits when my parents walked into their offices. So my parents decided to sidestep real estate agents and focus on other ways to buy a house, like reading newspaper obituaries. After all, a family in mourning might feel pressured to entertain a strong offer, regardless of the race of the bidder, as long as the money on the table was green. Ghoulish, but Belvin and Betty did what they had to do, and eventually things worked out for them.

In January 1961, they found a three-bedroom, two-story, Tudor Revival on a corner lot with a large yard, an open kitchen, a large limestone fireplace, and a finished basement with knotty pine paneling. After her first marriage, Mom, with two daughters, had been a little gun-shy about relationships when she'd met the handsome man from Alabama. As she watched Dad cut the real estate deal, she said she was reminded why she'd married him. When my parents showed up to make their offer, they saw discomfort on the white sellers' faces. Mom and Dad explained that they had been preapproved for a loan and could make a decent down payment. And just when they sensed that the sellers and their agent were about to bolt, Dad stood up and said, "Do you really want to lose a sure thing for only a possibility?" The sellers were close in age to my parents. I have since discovered that the husband came from a small town in southwest Minnesota. He was the son of an insurance salesman and had enlisted in World War II two months after my father joined the navy. The two men were discharged from the armed forces around the same time. I can imagine that Cecil Fuller may have looked at Belvin Norris and seen more than just a "Negro." Perhaps he also identified with a fellow veteran eager to use the G.I. Bill to pull himself and his family up.

In any case, the Fuller family said yes when so many others had said no. On February 1, 1961, Belvin and Betty Norris signed the deed to the largest house on the 4800 block of Oakland Avenue. My mother's sister advised her against buying so big a house. "It will just make it harder," Aunt Doris said. "Why give them another reason to judge you? They're going to say you think too highly of yourself. You know how they are." Mom wasn't having it. "I do think highly of myself, and I don't care if they know that. In fact, I prefer if they know that."

My parents moved in within a week, and the white families whose property line touched ours soon put their homes up for sale. Three who owned houses across from my parents' also decided to decamp. As my parents celebrated their new home with a picnic supper, amid boxes in the living room, their neighbors furiously burned the dial, calling each other, calling my folks' mortgage lender to complain, and eventually calling real estate agents to put their homes up for sale pronto. Mom says she watched the white flight with a mixture of anger and amusement. The desperation of her new neighbors to sell gave her an opportunity for a little mischief.

Every time a real estate agent pulled up with a prospective buyer, she would send my older sisters, Marguerite and Cindy, out to play in the yard. Or she would saunter out herself, holding her back or stretching her arms so anyone could plainly see that another child was on the way. That child was me. My sisters and I never knew any of this until recently, but now Mom loves telling the story. "I'd wait until they got inside the house and had time to check out the bedrooms and look inside the closets, and right about the moment I thought they were in the kitchen giving it a real good look-see, I'd say to myself: 'Showtime!'

"No matter what your older sisters were doing I'd tell 'em, time to get some fresh air. Go on. Go! Out in the yard. If the kids were at school I'd go outside myself and make sure they saw that I had a child on the way." She adds, "You couldn't count to ten before those people would be scurrying out the front door, back to their cars."

The family that lived next door had the hardest time unloading their property, even though their For Sale sign went up the very day my parents moved in. Three generations lived in the home, a grandmother, her son and daughter-in-law, and their children. They were "displaced persons" from Eastern Europe, and my mother told my older sisters never, ever to refer to them as DPs. Our next-door neighbors, however, saw no need for courtesy. The wife was a homemaker, a woman who nowadays might be referred to as a member of the sandwich generation because she was taking care of her elderly mother-in-law as well as her children. She had a heavy Eastern European accent and only one arm, and she used to usher her kids inside anytime my sisters stepped into the yard. My mother shakes her head in disbelief as she recalls how the woman would stand on her stoop, clutching her shoulder, as my parents carried groceries from the car. She would stare down my mother when she left for work. My mother would stare back and wave. I can see Mom gliding down the front steps with her smart black handbag and one of her classic "get with the program" smiles. Great day, isn't it?

The forlorn For Sale sign sat in front of the house for weeks. At one point, someone attached a flyer that read BEWARE. NEGRO NEIGHBORS, and the woman wailed so loudly that her cries ricocheted through our kitchen window. Sometimes I wonder: Shouldn't my mother have been the one moved to tears? But that was not her style.

My sisters were told to keep their distance from our neighbors. And usually they did. But an unfortunate incident occurred. The neighbors had a hardy little apple tree, and some of the branches reached into our yard. When my sisters plucked a few apples from the tree, the woman sent her husband over to ask them to cut it out. He seemed somewhat ashamed to have to carry out his wife's order. He and my father had achieved a measure of civility; they would exchange curt greetings while shoveling snow or cutting grass. Despite his discomfort, the husband's message was firm. For everyone's sake, leave the damn apples alone.

My sisters complied for a few days. But soon temptation was too strong. The moment Marguerite and Cindy plucked a few more apples, they were caught red-handed by the woman. Within minutes she stormed angrily out of her back door, chattering away in her native tongue. My sisters couldn't understand what she was saying, but they knew to get back inside the house, fast! The next day a landscaping crew chopped the tree down, creating a void in the nicely designed yard. When they finished the job, a smattering of red apples lay in our yard. "I told the kids, don't you dare touch those apples," my mother said. She finally went out and scooped the fruit up. She thought how nice it would be to put them in a basket lined with fresh gingham, or perhaps to bake them in a cobbler or a lattice-top pie, and deliver a gift at the doorstep of the furious woman next door. She thought about it. But instead she threw the apples away.

My mother's tough. Rock of Gibraltar tough. John Wayne tough. Minnesota-winter tough. She lives life on her own terms; she's an original. She has no patience for "woe is me." Once, years later, when we were vacationing on a cruise to Alaska, Mom struck up a friendship with a fellow passenger, who told her how she keeps things in perspective. "Everybody is somebody's pain in the ass," the woman said. "Today someone is getting on my nerves but tomorrow I am certain to bug the hell out of somebody else. That's just the way life works." Mom loved that. It explained so much. She adopted that phrase and added her own coda: "Life would be pretty boring if we all got along all of the time."

In retrospect, I can see how Mom's tough-as-nails exterior might keep people at bay, but she also has a wicked sense of humor and a laugh that commands you to join in the fun. Sometimes I think she has the heart of a cleric. People seek her wisdom and track her down for comfort. Social graces are of extreme importance to her. She raised "please and thank you" daughters in a "Hey, how ya doing?" culture. Now, as adults, we share her small obsessions with thank-you notes, table linens, guest books, and carefully planned menus. Social conventions shaped her views about decorum and the management of her home, but in almost every other way she's a woman who colors outside the lines.

Mom wasn't quite like all the other women in the neighborhood. She always seemed larger—not physically, though she's what you might call stately because her erect posture seems to add inches to her tall, lean frame. She turned gray early and refused to dye her hair. There was something about her that always seemed epic, like the larger-than-life characters we used to read about at night when she sat at the edge of my twin bed.

She reminded me of those prairie women who pushed the plows on the plains. In reality she, like my father, was a postal worker; she sallied out of the house each morning bearing her thermos as if it were a scepter. Our neighborhood was full of women who took no guff from their children, but Mother was a cut above the rest. She could turn you into Jell-O with one of her looks, which she used to great effect in and outside our home. She'd give the clerk at Kramarczuk's market a glance that would somehow compel him to pick out the best Warsaw ham from the refrigerator case. She'd narrow her eyes a bit when she spoke to my teachers, ensuring that my slight childhood speech impediment would not keep me from joining accelerated classes. And if my friends stepped out of line on her watch, she would fuss at them as if they were her own kids.

Never tell her that she can't do something. She is a two-time breast cancer survivor who has probably outlived the gray-haired doctor who crouched down in a hospital corridor thirty-some years ago to tell me that my mother might not see me graduate from high school. She proved the doctor wrong that day and beat the odds twenty-five years later, when cancer struck again. She showed him. She showed us all. She danced at my wedding, gave my daughter her first bath at the hospital, and wiped away joyful tears at both of my children's first communions.

One spring afternoon, she and I returned home after softball practice and froze when we heard hurried footsteps on the second floor. My older sisters had moved out by then. Dad was at work. Someone was in our house who did not belong there. My instinct was to flee and call the police from safety. Mom instead braced herself for a confrontation. She grew red with anger.

Weeks before, a burglar had broken in and had stolen my father's video equipment and a few pieces of Mom's costume jewelry. My mother and father were devastated by the violation—not just by the loss of property but by the notion that someone had been pawing through their things with abandon while they were off earning a living. They were unusually quiet at dinner after the break-in. They'd wait until I headed upstairs for bed; only then would I hear them pacing and fretting, wondering aloud who would have done such a thing. The theft ate away at my parents for weeks. Just when they'd started to relax and once again keep the bedroom windows open all night for fresh, cool air, another intruder was on the premises, wandering around in our private spaces.

Mom wasn't having it. She threw down the grocery bag, tossed her purse in my direction, and stormed toward the stairs. Before she got to the landing, a long-haired teenager came whooshing down, zoomed through the living room, and zipped right out the front door. The scene was almost comical. I never saw the look on his face, but all the blond hair flying this way and that reminded me of Saturday morning cartoons. Mom roared at the guy like a mama bear chasing a skunk from her den. Without blinking, she took off after him down the street, screaming at the burglar while punching the air with her fist. I wonder what that kid thought when he looked over his shoulder and saw a middle-aged black woman hoofing it in pursuit. She tired halfway down the block and put her hands to her knees as she tried to catch her breath. The long-haired kid hopped into the passenger side of a car waiting for him and sped off.

It was late afternoon, and the setting sun made Oakland Avenue look like a movie set. Shards of light bounced off windshields and the chrome handlebars of banana-seat bicycles. A group of kids halfway down the block, straddling their Sting-Ray bikes, watched the scene with utter amazement. Mom motioned to the uncomprehending kids to chase after the car to confirm the license plate number; she was so winded she couldn't yell anymore. I spied the whole thing from the safety of our front steps and knew that this would be the talk of the playground for weeks. Not that I minded. This was the mid-seventies, when blaxploitation films featured baaadass women, when *Get Christie Love* lit up our TV screens and we cheered in our beanbag chairs as Teresa Graves shouted, "You're under arrest, sugah!" every time she nabbed one of the bad guys.

Once Mom had huffed and puffed her way back into the house and started fixing our dinner, I overheard her on the phone talking to Aunt Doris, who by now lived a few blocks down Oakland Avenue. One of the first things she said was "Thank God he wasn't black; I'd have hunted him down and wrung his neck." I could very well imagine Aunt Doris, in her fashionable clothes, nodding her head while uttering her "you know it's" and "yes honey's." The exchange was memorable because at the time I wondered, Would our white neighbors, upon seeing the teenage hoodlum with his dirty-blond hair and carpenter pants, fleeing our house, ever say: "Christ, why did he have to be white?" Even then I knew the answer. Blacks often feel the dispiriting burden of being perceived willy-nilly as representing an entire race. The idea made my head hurt, and it still does if I dwell on it too much. To this day I have to tamp down anxiety when I step on a stage or into a studio. The notion that I can lift up others through stellar work or stall their progress by falling short has been drummed into me since childhood.

Whether the responsibility is an honor or a burden, I accept it as a fact of life. Whenever I feel the anxiety, I hear my parents: my father telling me, "Wake up and smell the opportunity," and my mother saying, "Snap out of it."

3
Aunt Jemimas

MOM LIKES TO PLAY a little game when people ask her where she's from. I'm a Minnesotan, she says, and if she is feeling really frisky she will stretch the *o* in *Minn-eh-sooooo-tan* to stress her bona fides. Then she waits for the inevitable next question: "But where did your people come from before they arrived here in Minnesota?" "Let me see," she says, stroking her chin. "I'd have to go back four generations." She sits back as their eyes grow wide with astonishment, which negates the inquiry.

Mom is proud to be fourth-generation Minnesotan. Hers was the only black family in the northern town of Alexandria. Her great-grandfather Austin Hopson and his son Fred were the town barbers. Though there were three other barbershops in Alexandria, theirs was favored by the town's professional class. When doctors, lawyers, and merchants came by for their daily straight-razor shave, the Hopson men would reach into a glass cabinet on the wall for the personalized shaving mug and brush of each patron.

Fred's daughter Ione was the only black child in her class throughout elementary and high school. She was a doe-eyed beauty with a lilting voice and a laugh that sounded like church bells. She used to tell us grandkids, "I decided to be happy." A darker choice would have been understandable. Ione Hopson led a lonely life. Her mother left home when Ione was a baby; it was chiefly her grandparents who raised her. And while she had close friends in school and in town, her social life became stunted as she got older, for everything began to revolve around dances and courtship. For Ione, there were no suitors. No dates. Even if she did have a girlhood crush on one of the farm boys or a young man who visited her father's shop for a buzz cut, she dared not talk about it to anyone.

Her luck changed, though, when a handsome black baseball player named Jinx rolled through town looking for steady work. Instead he found love. Jinx's birth name was Vernon, but no one ever called him that. At some point in his youth a friend had taken to calling him Bad News Brown because he always knew the latest gossip. Bad News Brown became Jinx. He was seventeen years older than Ione, but that didn't matter. Soon Jinx and Ione moved to St. Paul and, eventually, to Minneapolis, where they raised four children.

By the time I was in elementary school, Grandmother Ione had become a bit of a local celebrity, always receiving citations from the mayor or keys to the city for her volunteer work with senior citizens. When she died, in 1983, her obituary in the local newspaper ran under the headline "Queen Mother Ione Brown."

She founded the U-Meet-Us Senior Citizen Center in Minneapolis, a refuge for older people of color who didn't always feel welcome at other such centers run by churches and the government elsewhere in the city. There they not only socialized but availed themselves of senior citizens' programs. In the mid-seventies Grandma Ione was interviewed about her work for an oral history project. "We needed a place where we can be free," she said. Grandma explained that while the Twin Cities had easily moved toward integration, older people in nursing homes and senior citizens' centers were still holding on to antiquated notions. "The day still has not arrived when you get integrated and really feel like you are accepted," she noted. "Whether the seniors in my day were the products of the

Depression years or had to go to work, [they] had to live with traditions and what society was at the time. And after you reach a certain age . . . it is very hard to change."

I loved listening to my grandmother's stories about life in the north and all the characters who would come through her family's barbershop. When I was in college I interviewed her for a women's studies course and we spent hours talking about her life and her travels throughout the Midwest. Her stories were rich. Upon arrival she could immediately determine the relative prosperity of a town by the quality of the curtains blowing through open windows. And she would look for another sign as well, the one tucked in a window's corner and bearing the word TOURIST—code for homes that provided lodging and meals to blacks. I had been led to believe that she was traveling through all those small towns with Grandpa Jinx, a railroad postal clerk.

Only recently did I learn the real reason for her travels. My mother's brother Jimmy is a history buff who's caught the genealogy bug. He spends most of his time researching Minnesota history and family lore. From him, I learned that Grandpa Jinx had lived in a stationary boxcar for most of his childhood, around the turn of the last century. Jimmy also revealed that Grandma Ione had worked for Quaker Oats as a traveling Aunt Jemima. For years in the late 1940s and early 1950s, she dressed up in a hoop skirt and apron, with a bandanna on her head, and traveled to small midwestern towns touting Aunt Jemima pancake mix to farmwives. At first it was hard for me to comprehend what my uncle meant. Grandma Ione had always been about style and polish in her speech and dress, and in the way she would carefully braid her long silver hair, then pile it on her head, crownlike, as in Frida Kahlo's self-portraits. Like so many women her age, she often bustled around the house wearing an occasional do-rag and an apron.

But her head wrap was satin and covered well-coiffed hair, her apron serving to protect an elegant, church-worthy, pastel dress or skirt.

I thought my mother was going to throw me out of her condo when I asked her about Grandma's work. She hated the story as much as she hated my badgering her for details. She was horrified that I might one day share it with the world. "Write about that after I'm gone," she would say. I was testing our bond. She's now softened, and the shame she felt about Grandma Ione's work lessened the more we talked about it. She now says, "If you write about this, you better get it right and make sure people know not just what that symbol means right now but what it used to mean when they first rolled out all that mammy mess." She's softened, yes, but still I sense the tightness in her jaw, the coldness in her eyes—the withering stare on the back of my neck—even as I write this.

I want to be clear about something. My disbelief about my grandmother's work as a traveling Aunt Jemima had nothing to do with shame. I just couldn't see her in the role. But I was fascinated, imagining her wandering the Midwest, earning money by convincing white women to part with theirs, white women who treated her like a celebrity when she came to town. "Oh, she was a very big deal when she showed up in those towns," Jimmy said. "Remember, she was a small-town girl who never got to shine 'cause she was always the sole dark spot in class. If she was treated as special, it was because she was different. Not because she was smart or beautiful. I know a lot of people are ashamed of that image, but I am not. I know what that did for her. She put that costume on and she was a star."

All the same, as I try to picture her in her costume, I'm swamped by ambivalence. Yes, she earned money and small-town fame, but it's hard to connect the woman you love with the character denigrated over time, depicted as a devoted, dim-witted plantation slave, heavyset and happy with her lot. How do you extract your icon from that history? I found a picture of my grandmother in her hometown paper, under the headline "Only Negro Alexandria High Graduate Portrays Version of 'Aunt Jemima': Hundreds of Pancakes Served Here Friday by Former Ione Hopson."[1]

You can't exactly say she's smiling for the camera. Her expression is one I've seen before. Both my mother and her sister have shown it on many an occasion: the cock of the head, the tightly set eyes, and the pursed lips. The look on my mother's face is usually accompanied by a quip: "Ain't this some mess!" Grandma Ione seems to be throwing off more attitude in the picture than is expected from Aunt Jemima. Mammies are about self-sacrifice and earthly wisdom; they are never spiteful. Their proverbial kitchens are full of sugar, not vinegar.

Who knows what my grandmother was thinking when the newspaper's photographer showed up. In such a small town, the photographer more than likely would have been someone she knew, or the son or daughter of a former classmate or customer at the Hopson family barbershop. In a gingham dress, one kerchief around her neck, another colorful one tied around her head, she's holding a spatula. The lower half of her body is obscured by a giant griddle. In the background there are pancake-mix boxes emblazoned with the smiling Aunt Jemima logo. A poster on the wall says, "Wake up to a Real American Breakfast."

Grandma's hometown paper described her as a "charming woman of ample proportions" and reported that she was "proud and happy with her new role in life." She'd been "discovered" by the Quaker Oats Company while singing at the Bethesda Baptist Church in South Minneapolis and hired to cover a six-state region encompassing Minnesota, the Dakotas, Michigan, Iowa, and Wisconsin. The original Aunt Jemima, it was claimed, was in Chicago. "I just sort of pinch-hit for her," Ione said.

She never told me about having worked for Quaker Oats, so reading the story was like listening to her speaking to me from the grave. She seems to be saying, Don't be ashamed for me, because I am not. She said her aim was to give Americans a favorable opinion of her people: "I'm a public representative of my race. I get the opportunity to meet little white children, children in small towns who have never ever seen a Negro before. I try to leave them with the best impression I can." She said she also tried to leave "a little touch of Christianity wherever I go." "All day long as I make pancakes for the good people I meet everywhere I sing church hymns and spirituals."

That struck home: my grandmother used to sing and hum to herself when she made pancakes for us, but it is odd to learn that she'd done the same thing for white customers who likely saw her as just one of many Aunt Jemimas who assumed the role of the happy-go-lucky, eager-to-please slave on the pancake box. My grandmother was an eloquent speaker—she won an oratorical contest in her high school but was unable to perform at the state level because Alexandria didn't want to send a "Negro representative." This was also something she'd kept to herself, a story I learned only when I came across an oral history by one of her high school classmates who'd talked about her hometown pancake demonstration. Grandma may have had a beautiful voice and lovely speech, but when you picked up a copy of *Ladies' Home Journal* or *Good Housekeeping* in the 1940s and 1950s, you were confronted with advertisements for the pancake mix that made Aunt Jemima sound like a buffoon. Aunt Jemima print campaigns then were essentially unchanged from those in the 1920s: "Lawsee! Folks sure cheer for fluffy, energizing Aunt Jemima Pancakes." Or: "Happyfyin' Aunt Jemima Pancakes. Sho' sets folks singin'!"

Aunt Jemima today is a silent spokeswoman, conveniently rendered moot by a corporation that finds itself in a delicate position, holding on to a valuable trademark widely recognized but historically offensive. The invention of Chris Rutt and Charles Underwood of the Pearl Milling Company, the character first appeared on pancake boxes in the 1890s, inspired by a popular minstrel song of the era. It was a gimmick and a good one, helping usher in an era of convenience cooking while playing to underlying racial nostalgia for the days when slaves fed the family and cared for the children.

Rutt and Underwood were better marketers than businessmen, and their company was purchased by R. T. Davis, who took the gimmick one step further by hiring a black spokeswoman named Nancy Green to portray Aunt Jemima at public events. A large and gregarious woman, Green had been born into slavery and had moved to Chicago to work for a well-known judge. Her debut at the 1893 World's Fair created an immediate sensation. It is said that she served more than a million pancakes during the fair's six-month run, and her catchphrase "I'se in town, honey" was popularized around the country.

Even as she served up pancakes, Green told stories of her life on the plantation. Prompted by R. T. Davis, she said she was the legendary cook of Louisiana plantation owner Colonel Higbee—a total fabrication. As the story went, her pancakes were the envy of the South, but she would never give up her recipe. Quaker Oats eventually purchased Davis's company, and the image and the myth of Aunt Jemima grew, the result of a massive ad campaign that featured novelistic text and painting by N. C. Wyeth.

J. Walter Thompson, once New York's largest ad agency, created a series that, historian Maurice Manring says, "turned Aunt Jemima from a trademark into a real Southern Cook," the story unfolding in full-page spreads that tried to bridge the gap between the Old South and modern notions of convenience and hospitality.[2] Wyeth and J. Walter Thompson adman James Webb Young were informed by what they would later call "the romantic school of advertising," their titles, text, and museum-quality illustrations dripping with drama and southern sentimentality.

One ad, called "Grey Morn," depicted downtrodden Confederate soldiers on the run, noting, "For two days the general and his orderly had been cut off from their troops: for two days, so the story goes, they had lain hidden in the bushes on the Mississippi's bank. Northern troops were everywhere, it seemed. No venture could be made by day, even for food. Only at night they dared move." The ad copy goes on to explain, in breathless prose, how the two soldiers found their way to the river, where they spotted a little cabin with smoke rising from the chimney. As they crept closer they heard a robust voice: "You chilluns pestah th' life out o' po' ol' mammy with yo' everlastin' appetite fo' pancakes!" Another ad shows former soldiers returning to find the woman who had saved them from near capture by Union troops: "We learned afterward that the mammy was Aunt Jemimah: befoah the wah cook in the family of one Cun'l Higbee, who owned a fine plantation heah and that she, in those days, known all ovah the South fo' huh cookin' skill, specially fo' huh pancakes."[3]

It is impossible to imagine an ad like that in a popular women's magazine today. As Manring, the author of *Slave in a Box: The Strange Career of Aunt Jemima,* notes, the ads sold "the promise that the buyer could appropriate the leisure, beauty, and racial and class status of the plantation South by purchasing a box of pancake flour." Not pancakes but a way of life was being sold.

Nancy Green, the original Aunt Jemima, died in 1923, after she was struck by a car in Chicago. Since then several women have been avatars of Aunt Jemima, among them Anna Robinson, Edith Wilson, Aylene Lewis, and Tess Gardella, a white Italian-

American actress who portrayed a blackface Aunt Jemima on-stage, the radio, and film. Gardella, who weighed more than four hundred pounds, is buried under a headstone with this inscription:

BELOVED SISTER
1898 THERESA 1950
"AUNT JEMIMA"
In God's Care

Quaker Oats claims that it does not keep a record of the dozens of women who worked as regional Aunt Jemimas—women like Grandma Ione or Rosie Lee Moore of Texas or Rosa Washington Riles of Ohio. The "pinch hitters," as my grandmother called them. According to Manring, the existence of such a record is highly unlikely, as most of these women were hired by district affiliates or local salespeople. "There is clear evidence that there were a lot of these women," Manring says. "They would go to county fairs, high schools, women's clubs, events like that. They apparently did what amounted to barn-storming from town to town." My mother's response? "Ain't that something? She claimed them and sold their product and probably took a lot of flak we'll never know about. And they decide they don't want to claim her. Now who is the saint and who is the slave in that picture? They appear to be slaves to the bottom line." The Aunt Jemima campaign has been fabulously successful. Quaker Oats dominates the market for pancake mix, as well as frozen waffles and French toast, and ranks second only to Log Cabin in syrup sales. Its bottom line is just fine.

My grandmother's work created a complex legacy for her heirs. Uncle Jimmy is the exception. Most of her grandchildren, like me, had no idea Grandma was once an Aunt Jemima. My mom and her sister, who remember the period all too well, are not so much embarrassed by her work as by the caricature she represented. It stings. They remember the boycott threats and the NAACP's open letters calling for an end to the degrading trademarked image. Mom and Aunt Doris can recall a time when blacks were called "hankerchief heads"—on par with "Uncle Tom"—and they understand that the insult could have easily been hurled at their own mother. And they turned the other cheek when people did say disparaging things about Ione Brown's line of work.

Uncle Jimmy says Grandma was aware of the backbiting but didn't talk much about it. Once when a neighbor quipped about her work, Grandma Ione told the woman she didn't have time to discuss the matter but would be happy to do so if the woman would join her later at the soup kitchen where she volunteered. That shut the woman up regarding Grandma's stint as Aunt Jemima.

My children see the friendly black woman on the pancake box smiling at them and have no idea of the tortured history behind that smile. The Aunt Jemima they're growing up with is a far cry from the woman whose provenance and speech are rooted in slavery. Aunt Jemima has had a series of highly publicized makeovers. First the do-rag was dropped, in favor of a plaid headband; now she has no headdress whatsoever. Today Aunt Jemima looks like a member of the local church council. She's got a perm with soft, gray-flecked curls, and she wears pearl earrings and a dainty lace Peter Pan collar right out of a Laura Ashley catalog. The bug-eyed smile is gone, replaced instead by a loving grin. Aunt Jemima demammified.

But demammified is not the same as destigmatized. In the mid-nineties my oldest sister, Marguerite, was in the hospital recovering from a heart ailment that would eventually take her life. She and my mother were chitchatting and watching television when the doctor approached on his rounds. Until then he'd earned high marks from our family for his sense of humor and his sensitivity in breaking bad news. But that afternoon he crossed a line. While gazing at his chart he told my sister, "You look like the lady on the pancake box." My mother said she was so wounded by his remark that she wanted to cuss him out, but instead she composed herself, hoping that her calm might alleviate my sister's humiliation.

The doctor's comment illustrates the quandary for Quaker Oats. It can modernize Aunt Jemima all it wants, but she will still drag her baggage around. Even as my mother did her best to forget the doctor's insult, Quaker Oats was struggling to relaunch its brand. Aunt Jemima got her perm and pearl earrings in 1989. By 1994, ad executives were trying to figure out how to make her come alive without conjuring up antebellum imagery. With the new catchphrase "Alive and Cookin'," the company was considering using a celebrity spokesperson to enhance the brand—one, however, not required to portray Aunt Jemima. "Due to the heritage and admitted baggage of the equity, the spokesperson for Aunt Jemima should be a strong independent African American woman, well-liked and respected," wrote brand manager Louise Wolf in a 1993 memo.[4]

The company had hired a large New York ad agency, Jordan, Case, McGrath & Taylor. It also sought outside consulting from the late Caroline Jones, who at the time ran the nation's premier African American ad agency. Decidedly against employing a spokesperson, Jones suggested that the company was oblivious to the world around them. "White people may have long forgotten the slaves of old, but no Black person can," Jones wrote.

All the same, Bruce Guidotti, an executive vice president for JCMT's Client Services Division, argued for a celebrity like Tina Turner, Robert Guillaume of *Benson* fame, or Gladys Knight. He wrote: "Aunt Jemima is a *person* (not an institution), Aunt Jemima is a food *expert,* a *friend* who can help me make [a] breakfast offering that I am absolutely certain will please me and my family. If we don't in the context of our campaign supply a personality as the vehicle for this message, it leaves open to interpretation who and what this person is like. . . . The worst is that they will supply their own interpretation, and if that is anachronistic and negative, we're in trouble."

Later, another JCMT adman, Peter Mitchell, suggested that the company go on the offensive. In a memo to Quaker Oats, he wrote, "There are some African Americans (both 'opinion leaders' as well as everyday folks) who resent the Aunt Jemima trademark and really don't want to see it advertised no matter what the campaign line is. We simply can't be held hostage by these people, but need to take steps to help ensure they keep their feelings to themselves."

The tender feelings of black consultants aside, the company hired Gladys Knight for a series of commercials in which her grandchildren swooned over delicious Aunt Jemima pancakes. She and the company received blistering reviews, but sales, including those captured from black consumers, continued to rise.

The internal Quaker Oats debate is well documented in "Aunt Jemima Is Alive and Cookin': An Advertiser's Dilemma of Competing Collective Memories," a scholarly paper written by Judy Foster Davis of Eastern Michigan University. Its most fascinating aspect is the tension concerning the word *alive* in the catchphrase "Alive and Cookin'." When Caroline Jones was asked to quietly collect views from black opinion makers, nearly everyone she spoke to zeroed in on that word. "My goodness, I hope not" was the consensus, she said. But that is precisely the point Quaker Oats was trying to make. The company wanted to capitalize on the food expert who is also a friend, but a friend represented by a happy slave who'd refused to give up her secret recipe to all those southern belles who used to flit around her kitchen. Quaker Oats wanted to have its cake and eat it too.

When the Gladys Knight ad campaign was launched in

1994, the catchphrase was changed from "Alive and Cookin' " to "Now You're Cooking." I imagine a conference room full of well-dressed black and white ad executives, everyone leaning back and uttering a sigh of relief once they've settled on a race-neutral line to sell a race-imbued product. Recently, in response to my query, Quaker Oats detailed what it wants us all to know: "The Aunt Jemima brand has been around for more than 115 years and continues to stand for warmth, nourishment and trust—qualities you'll find in loving moms from diverse backgrounds who care for and want the very best for their families. The Aunt Jemima brand continues to stand for great taste and the tradition of helping moms provide a wholesome breakfast for the whole family." The company had no interest in talking about what else the Aunt Jemima brand might stand for.

Nonetheless, Americans both black and white continue to hold on to the Aunt Jemima image. For white Americans in particular, she is a trope for their complex feelings of love and guilt toward black servants and slaves. Blacks continue to see her as a constant reminder never to let down their lest-we-forget guard. Some black Americans, including the celebrities Bill Cosby and Whoopi Goldberg, obsessively collect mammy memorabilia. My own mother, who had long held conflicted feelings about Grandma Ione's work, kept an Aunt Jemima cookie jar on her kitchen counter and an old slave advertisement on the wall. "We need to be more like the Jews," she says. "Instead of trying to forget, we need to never forget so we can draw strength from that which we have overcome."

In Natchez, Mississippi, on Highway 61, you can grab lunch inside a thirty-three-foot-tall building designed to look like a giant Aunt Jemima. The restaurant sits inside her wide pink hoopskirt. Above there used to be a massive, bosomy concrete woman holding a tray. She had wide pink lips, a red bandanna, and horseshoes for earrings. Like the Aunt Jemima on the pancake box, she, too, has gotten a makeover: her skin is now lighter, she's slimmed down a bit, and her chest is smaller. She even appears to be wearing eye shadow and blush. The restaurant is called Mammy's Cupboard, and its current owner, Linda Moore, says there is no reason to take offense at the building or its name.

"At one point," Moore notes, "Mammy was a slave. You could say there is not a lot of honor in that. But she was also the person who nurtured families and raised children. There is honor in everything you do and [for those who] have young people in their care. You have a crying child. Who are they going to run to? Nine times out of ten, they are going to run to their mammy. I am not trying to gloss this up. A lot of people have had maids and housekeepers and helpers who have shown them more love and given them more wisdom than any member of their real-life family. I want people to look at her [the building] and see that. Not some ugly stereotype."

"Sometimes," Moore adds, "I don't understand why black folks don't claim her, because she was theirs first. She's still theirs, isn't she?"

As I listen to Linda Moore I'm reminded of something I heard from Horace Huntley at the Birmingham Civil Rights Institute. I asked him what he thought of the symbol of Aunt Jemima today and he got surprisingly emotional: "You know, it's obviously looked upon as a caricature, but I've really never looked at it that way because she looks like my grandmother. However, it's like discussions you may have—you might have a joke in the family about a black person that you would tell. . . . If a white person's there, we would not tell the joke . . . but if they are not present, we can have a grand time."

He went on: "I guess that's the double consciousness that W.E.B. DuBois talks about. How Aunt Jemima looks like Grandmama, and she was the most intelligent person that I have ever known who walked the face of the earth, although she couldn't read or write, but now if this white person sees her, then I'm perceiving what their vision is of that individual. And I love her, and I think they're saying that this demeans. That's my perception. They are looking at her as demeaning black women, totally, where I'm looking at it as being with endearment. . . . We've allowed someone else to control who we are. And even who we perceive that we are."

Sometimes it seems as if the ghost of Aunt Jemima lives at my local Target; she pops up in the strangest ways when I'm there, whether I'm fighting with my children about whether or not we should buy Aunt Jemima pancake mix or fielding questions from others with their own Aunt Jemima dilemmas. Long before I knew about my grandmother, I was heading toward the baking aisle at Target one day when I heard a redheaded kid ask his mother, "Mommy, who is Aunt Jemima?" I made the mistake of glancing in his mother's direction. The pert blonde raised her eyebrows as if to invite me to answer her son. I arched my own eyebrows in alarm. I walked away determined not to go there with a stranger.

Now if the kid were to ask me the question, I would say, "Aunt Jemima was my grandmother" and let him and his mother ponder that. I respect Grandma Ione for having taken a job, despite being haunted by stigma, and having used it to lift her family up. We judge Aunt Jemima and ourselves by what we see reflected in the mirror of her history.

4

The Garden

GRADUALLY, ALL BUT ONE OF our neighbors' homes were purchased by or rented to other black families. The whites bolted for the suburbs or other all-white enclaves in the Twin Cities. Many suffered significant losses in their rush to sell. Those who could find no buyer rented their homes, having gotten used to the idea of being landlords to black tenants. That's how integration came to the 4800 block of Oakland Avenue. Despite a chilly reception at first, our family developed deep and meaningful friendships with the white families farther down the block who had decided to stay, and with others who would later move to our little rainbow community.

Perhaps because they had started this real estate revolt, my parents made sure that the white families who didn't move would never have legitimate complaints about their black neighbors. The Norris family led by example. Not only was the snow always shoveled; cars were sparkling clean, and children were well mannered and well dressed. "You never know who's watching," Mom would say. So even if we were playing with dolls in the basement or heading out to weed the garden, we always looked put together. Hair pressed. Clothes ironed. Shoes spit-polished. Mud wiped instantly from our tennis shoes. We didn't just emulate the all-American white families in the Coca-Cola commercials—we tried to top them.

If you had run into Belvin and Betty Norris during one of our vacations, you might have thought you'd bumped into the king and queen of the black bourgeoisie. My parents were not pretenders to a lifestyle above their station. In their own little way they saw themselves as sartorial activists doing their part to chip away at stereotypes about Black America. "Don't you know we have to undo what Hollywood does?" Dad would say. "They leave folks thinking that we're all pimps or poor or dim in the head. Well, when people see us, and see people who have pride in how they carry themselves, people who work every day and take care of their families, then maybe they will think twice about all that mess they see on TV."

Mom and Dad were obsessive about looking clean and stylish and sophisticated because they lived in a society that perpetuated the notion that black people, in the main, were none of those things. Yes, Belvin and Betty wore uniforms or simple, sensible clothing when they marched off to work at the post office. But before taking to the road, they'd reach into the other side of the closet. They didn't own a lot of clothes, but when they bought "civilian wear," they bought quality. Dad favored belted, safari-style jackets or dark blazers with gold buttons, a look he augmented with ribbed turtlenecks and jauntily tied paisley ascots. For a time he went through a links phase, wearing the brightly colored golf cardigans favored by such singers as Perry Como and Andy Williams.

Mom was always a half step ahead of what passed for chic in South Minneapolis. If she could see it, she could sew it. And so she sported looks first shown in movies or on television shows, long before they wound up on local racks. By the time Twin Cities fashionistas embraced gaucho pants or the return of the peplum jacket, Mom had already moved on to something else. "Always look for the line," she'd say. "Imagine the silhouette. Does it enhance your figure or take away from it?" The women in our family tend to be narrow-shouldered and broad through the beam. When the salesladies would say things like "Follow me, we have wonderful shifts that work for pear-shaped women," Mom would quip to me, "I wonder if she has something for women shaped more like a Chianti bottle." Mom liked nipped waists, beautiful fabric, well-tailored slacks.

Both Mom and Dad loved "glad rags," and vacation gave them a chance to strut their stuff. I didn't understand why, and I still chuckle when I view home movies of us dressed to the nines at the zoo or an amusement park or touring the Canadian Rockies, while other tourists are, for the most part, in athletic gear. My father would never dream of showing up at Disney World in cutoff shorts and tire-soled sandals. When I begged and pleaded to wear my favorite Britannia bell-bottom jeans strategically torn at the knee and frayed at the hem, he stood at the door, arms crossed, calmly shaking his head from side to side. "Ain't gonna happen, Mickey," he'd say. "Dress like you're going somewhere."

He would often wait in the foyer in his Easter-egg-colored Munsingwear shirt with the little penguin on the pocket and his carefully creased pants, prepared to lead his family out of the house as if headed to somebody's fashion shoot. Mom's handbag would match her shoes, and would be stylishly in sync with the scarf she always carried to tie around her head, her neck, or the handle of her purse, like a sepia-toned Babe Paley. When we walked through a hotel lobby, Dad would doff his cap at other guests padding around in flip-flops and Hush Puppies. I would hear them whispering and sense them staring at us as we passed.

My parents spoke loudly in other ways. My father, for instance, let his flowers do the talking. He was a passionate gardener. I don't quite know where he got his green thumb, because his parents were not yard people. Back in Alabama, my father's father, Belvin senior, was a hunter who always had two or three hound dogs. My grandparents' wood-frame bungalow sat on raised cinder blocks; the hounds slept under the house. They ate about as well as people, and they tore up the yard with little or no consequence. I don't remember many bushes or flowers in the front yard, but the few plants in the backyard produced food for the table: beans, tomatoes, peppers, collards, polk salad, peaches, and figs. So it is hard for me to imagine when or how my father became fluent in the language of roses. Maybe he just picked it up along the way or inherited some plants from the previous owner of our house in Minnesota.

Year after year, my father and mother worked to transform our yard into a Victorian oasis adorned with roses, peonies, bleeding hearts, and black-eyed Susans, all carefully arranged inside a white picket fence, freshly painted every spring. South Siders would go out of their way to stroll by the house or drive past slowly with their windows down, waving at my father as he sprayed his "darlings" (that's what he called his roses). Or they would crane over the fence as they spoke to my mom, trying to figure out her secret fertilizer.

Though pretty, the yard sometimes took on a sharp odor, depending on that year's experimental fertilizer. Cayenne pepper, bone meal, eggshells, and fish oil—my mom tried all of them to perfect her gardening. Her concoctions were neighborhood lore. My playmates' mothers were always asking me to share Mom's secrets, and while I am now an avid gardener, at the time I could say in all honesty that I had no idea what they were talking about. I took no interest in the freakish sight of eggshells marinating in an empty mayonnaise jar next to the kitchen sink, or bags of fertilizer made from fish, blood, or bone meal stacked up in the garage. My parents called it their victory garden. Unfortunately, as carefully as they tended it, they had less success cultivating a strong relationship between themselves. By the time I got to junior high school, their marriage had collapsed, for reasons I never understood until I started writing this book.

Mom moved eight blocks down the street on Oakland Avenue. Dad and I stayed in the Tudor house with its lush garden. He picked up the pieces and turned our house into a protective cocoon. The flowers in the yard were part of his armor. Dad tried even harder to keep up appearances, determined that the vitality of the garden would hide the death of his marriage. I was and still am baffled by my father, as I think of him in this stormy period. I am amazed by the scant upheaval of it all. I was only a few years older than my own kids are now. We were a broken working-class family in the 1970s. No housekeepers or maids or nannies, but ours was always a spotless house.

Mom made a deliberate decision to stay in the neighborhood when she moved out, purchasing a run-down but nearby house so she could hover around the edges during my teenage years while she renovated her new property. She and Dad settled into a friendly relationship. They showed up as a twosome to all my games and chaperoned school events together. We even celebrated holiday meals together. The whole thing was so weirdly civilized that I doubt most of my teachers even knew that Mr. and Mrs. Norris were no longer officially a couple.

I've always found my parents' marriage enigmatic. There was the romance, then the partnership, then the breakup. When they split I was of an age when I'd just begun to think in rudimentary ideas about intimate relationships. Most of what I gleaned came from magazine articles or eavesdropping on my sisters. They were ten and twelve years older than me, and they were fabulously entertaining to a preteen kid. Their clothes. Their music. The dance moves they tried out. The hair tape one of them would wear to bed the night before a school dance, so that a little curl would dangle from her hairline and cling to her cheek. The young men they swooned over while giggling in the basement. But Marguerite and Cindy had moved away by the time my parents' marriage started to crumble.

Looking back, I missed the cues. I knew there were tensions and occasional arguments. Mom spent a lot of time away from home, working her side job at the post office library or bowling in a league; Dad often whiled away hours at his brother

Woody's house. The chatter of late-night TV was sometimes interrupted by the clink of bottles—a search for small comfort in drink. There were no screaming matches or explosive fights, at least not when I was around. Belvin and Betty just seemed to glide to the finish line. One day they were living under the same roof; one day they weren't. I now know they must have orchestrated the transition to play out so smoothly. They must have made arrangements for me to be absent when they moved my mother's suitcases to her new home, or conveniently to be at a sleepover when they carried out her book collection and favorite pieces of furniture. And my extended family was in on the conspiracy of silence. No one ever talked to me about my parents' divorce beyond asking, "Ya doin' all right, Mickey?"

Over time, I, too, joined the conspiracy. Only once did I ask each of my parents what happened to their marriage, and on both occasions, I learned not to ask again. As I speculated about the reasons for their breakup, I could only conclude that their work schedules had done them in. Mom worked early mornings by choice so she could be home when I returned from school. Dad worked eight to five. I figured they'd been like ships passing, for even as Mom was retiring at night, Dad was putting on his slippers to relax at the end of a long day.

Only in the course of writing this book have I finally been able to talk to my mother about her decision to leave our home. It is not painful in the ways I'd expected, which is not to say it didn't hurt. As I listen to my mother, the picture of my father that emerges is very different from the one I have clung to for all these years. The man who turned our home into an island of calm was also a man compelled to disdain all outside forces that might disrupt his domestic serenity. I thought my father had learned to exercise extreme discipline to rein in those things he could control, in order to rise above those things he could not. As I hear my mother's side of the story, his control was something less virtuous and much more like the bars of a cage. Mom did not relish sharing her story. She has always known how close I was to my father. She did not want to tarnish my memories of him. It's an understatement to say that I had to coax her to talk. Beg her. Decades after the breakup, I finally feel closer to the truth. Or at least her truth.

Much of the tension between my parents during that time is crystallized in Mom's mind by something that happened at a party. She tells an anecdote time and again whenever she describes that period. "We're talking about this and that and the subject of chitterlings came up and I said I don't bring chitterlings in my kitchen," Mom says, nearly spitting out the word: *chitlins.* "I just don't do it. Don't like the way they smell. Don't like to clean them. I just don't want to mess with them at home."

The first time she tells me this, she crosses her hands in her lap and looks me dead in the eye. "Your Dad said: 'You'd cook them if I told you to.' " This might seem like a minor infraction, the kind of thing that might lead to shouting in the car on the way home or maybe Mom's giving Dad the cold shoulder for a week. Not something that would sink a marriage, prompting a mother to leave her teenage daughter behind. But I can see from Mom's look that she'd borne a much deeper insult and, more than likely, not for the first time.

"We were in a circle of people and it was like he had to show them who's the boss. That was the beginning of the end. He was willing to humiliate me. He was willing to do that so our friends would see he had power inside his house. I don't know what hurt me more, the embarrassment or the realization that your father needed respect that badly." My father was a gentle man. He rarely raised his voice and was never violent. But for all her toughness, Mom had a soft underside that was easily wounded by words. Her needs clashed with his. It was as simple as that. But it also had to be complicated and unbearable. Why else would a mother flee her family?

My mother's cheeks seem to sink when she tries to explain how my father, despite his efforts, was not the partner she'd needed while struggling through her first bout with cancer. Her admission was like a stab to my gut. I remember my father doting on Mom during those long weeks when she slept on a cot in the living room because she was too weak to walk up the stairs. I remember Dad carrying trays of soup to her bedside, and going downtown to get the Sunday *New York Times* for her. He fixed her sponge baths and emptied her bedpans. But emotional support is as important as physical health in combating cancer, and Mom apparently enjoyed neither. "After my breast cancer your father just did things that were . . . well." Her voice trails off. "He talked about what *he'd* lost." I'd heard enough.

The man she was describing was not the man I'd known. I'd been living with confusion and anger for decades, for I'd assumed that Mom had just run out on Dad to live life by her own rules. I didn't know that she'd thought she was running for her life.

At some point in the telling Mom shakes her head and concedes, "I'm no angel"—this is as close to an explanation of her detachment and departure as I've ever heard from her. And after yearning for some kind of explanation all these years, it turns out to be more than I can take. In sum, Mom's account of our life on Oakland Avenue is this: Dad, who had had so little control over the circumstances of his early years, made sure to have absolute control at home. And for a woman as independent as Betty Norris, their marriage was bound to meet with extreme turbulence. Just because I didn't hear the shouting doesn't mean all was well. He tried to bend her will; she succeeded in breaking his heart. But we all survived and moved on. Dad and Mom both had other loving relationships, and they maintained their friendship until he passed away. Mom was with Dad the night he slipped into a coma. Deep in her eyes, you still see a faint flicker when she talks about Dad's essential goodness.

"Here's the thing about your father," Mom says. "He put family first. And he never wanted a handout from anyone. He worked hard. He saved his money. He liked nice things, but only if he felt that he'd earned them. And he wasn't ashamed of being black. And he was not afraid of black women." She pauses for effect, then says: "As long as they did what he said." We both fall over laughing—the kind of knowing laughter I now share with my husband, Broderick. The sudsy giggles I enjoy with my children and closest girlfriends.

I am grateful for this gift from my parents, who could not make a go of their marriage but still managed to teach me the importance of love. And the importance of grace, for it would have been easy for my father to nurse anger at the woman who abandoned her home and her child. Easy for him to have tried to influence me to partake in his umbrage. Instead, he kept a place for her at our table, so to speak, even as she lived under a different roof. I learned from both Mom and Dad that everything in life is enriched by sharing it with someone. I gleaned that from the years they spent together and the years they decided to be together cheering me on, while living eight blocks apart.

When Mom left, Dad slunk deeper into himself. He picked up the slack without complaining, but he also read all the time. I would come downstairs at night and find him immersed in Kahlil Gibran or the plays of George Bernard Shaw. Now that his wife was gone, he and I rarely ate at the dining room table. The two of us would have dinner at the kitchen counter, a portable TV in the corner nook. The setting had changed, but the rituals continued, for the most part. There was always food in the fridge and hot meals for supper. Dad now cooked most of our meals, and I took on the rest. No takeout. Little or no fast food.

Mom helped out some, but she and Dad tried to keep their distance during these tenuous times. They also held their tongues. It would be thirty years before I would have a hint as to why my mother had simply said "enough" and bolted from our house to purchase her own. Dad and I did okay around the house, but ironing stumped us both. My mother had had her own technique to put a certain snap in Dad's postal uniform, placing damp shirts in the freezer for fifteen minutes before smoothing them out with a hot iron. When Dad asked me to do the same, I refused, sputtering something awful like "I'm just a kid, not a wife!" I did my household chores, but the presumptuous independence that comes with adolescence provoked me to draw the line at ironing. I was a confused teenager testing how far I could go. He had every right to slap me. He didn't. Eventually, I gave in, but despite my best efforts, I couldn't match my mom's skill at nailing down the collar and smoothing out the postal patches without completely flattening the embroidery. Still, it was the trying that counted.

The yard that had been our childhood playground became my private retreat as I grew older. My friends and I used to sit in plaid lounge chairs, slather ourselves with Hawaiian Tropic oil, and bask in the sun for hours, passing around Fresca and *Seventeen* magazines. My father never said as much, but he must have thought me ridiculous: lounging was a patent waste of time; suntan oil, a waste of good money. He must have found it all confounding; he'd grown up at a time when black newspaper ads promoted skin-lightening creams and "Negro" girls were told to stay out of the sun! Sometimes I would stretch out by myself in the yard, arms and legs spread as if making a snow angel. I'd look up at the clouds and listen to distant car radios, or I'd close my eyes, better to hear the buzz of insects, the fizz of my soda's carbonation, the hiss of the wind. I still love the sound of shimmering leaves, as relaxing as a cool drink after a long day's work. Back when I spent hours sunning and day-dreaming, if I had truly centered myself and listened even more intensely, I might have also heard a gossamer whisper: the flowers, speaking for my father, saying to his neighbors, "I belong."

5
Alabama

I ALWAYS WONDER HOW a young man could go through his early life with a nickname like "Honey." That's what everyone called my father in Birmingham. Honey. Though, to get it right you had to let the first syllable hang a bit: "Hu-uh-nee." It seemed too sweet a name for a young man unless he was a blues singer or a boxer. Dad was neither. He was the second youngest of six sons from the Ensley neighborhood of Birmingham, Alabama. Anyone who questioned his nickname would quickly have to confront a rambunctious fraternity. All of the Norris men were tall, thin, and talkative—quick with a punch line and, if necessary, even quicker with a sharp left hook. You had to deal with all of them if you tried to take one on. And you had to have a thick skin and a keen wit to run with the Norris boys. They teased and ribbed and challenged one another constantly. They called it signifyin'. They'd talk about the size of your girlfriend's behind and expect you to laugh. They'd crack on your clothing or your eyeglasses or your skin tone and then wait, with antic anticipation, for you to swat it right back with another wisecrack. And there always was another one: "Man, where'd you get them shoes? Don't you know that Santa's been callin' 'cause he wants his boots back!"

The ribbing could go on and on for hours, and it usually did. And when it went one step too far with a joke about a wife or, worse, somebody's mama, that was when my father would step up and talk down the offended party. "C'mon now . . . you know we're just playing. You got to signify to qualify and, man, you more than qualified. You hung right in there," Belvin would say, draping his arm around the shoulder of the aggrieved fellow to steer him away from the front porch, away from his brothers shaking with laughter while celebrating their verbal dexterity. Dad would keep that fellow moving along, away from the snickering and merriment. All the while, he'd be looking over his shoulder to shush his brothers, quietly sharing in the pride of the takedown. Dad was always a bit of a square, and it took extra effort for him to riff like a hep cat. "Man, you got to shake it off," he'd say. "We're just havin' fun. You know the story. We all get a cut, we all *get* cut. Sometimes you gotta laugh to keep from crying."

A clan of six, the Norris brothers were thick as thieves yet devoted as apostles to an inviolate creed: good times allowed only after a day's hard work. They were very much their father's sons.

My grandfather had worked in the steel mills and the coal mines until age forced him to retire, after which he occupied himself with neighborhood odd jobs. My grandmother Fannie worked too, as a nurse's aide, logging a short shift after she put her sons to bed. Belvin and Fannie were savers and strivers. They stood out in Ensley because they owned their own home and managed to keep new cars in the garage. Grandpa Belvin turned those cars into a business, shuttling people to and fro for money. For years, though, he refused to drive to church on Sunday mornings, a custom some neighbors believed he adopted from the city's large Orthodox Jewish population. Jewish merchants ran most of Birmingham's department stores and nearly all the shops in Ensley. For the Orthodox, driving on the Sabbath is taboo because starting an engine is akin to lighting a fire; the Torah forbids kindling a fire on the holy day of rest.

Grandpa Belvin was tickled by the rumor and never did much to quell it. But his sons knew the real reason he didn't drive on Sunday. He liked to walk the half mile to church with his wife, Fannie, by his side and his six sons in single file behind him like sentries. More than the deed to the house, or the car in the driveway, or the windup mantel clock or upright Zenith radio, more than the three black suits he owned (two more than most men on his block), my grandfather treasured this ritual of walking with his family to church.

In my mind's eye I can see Belvin and Fannie leading their sons to the First Baptist Church on Avenue G, nodding at neighbors, walking slowly but with purpose in the Alabama heat, gently waving fans glued to Popsicle sticks. I see my grandfather, one hand in his pocket, the other intertwined with his wife's. And I see six boys ambling behind them, all with slightly knock-kneed gaits, poking and elbowing each other as they secretly pass mints and chewing gum back and forth. The scene is easy to imagine, for on two occasions, the boys returned to First Baptist to bury their parents. As often happens at funerals, children revert to their earliest family roles. The jokester. The pacifist. The cheapskate. There they were, middle-aged men, each with one of Grandma Fannie's lace hankies in his breast pocket, passing Chiclets and breath spray around. They stood in the church vestibule, joshing with one another about their expanding waistlines and receding hairlines, signifyin' before assuming their pallbearer duties. Sometimes you do have to laugh to keep from crying.

I spent part of every summer in Alabama from when I was in swaddling clothes until I entered junior high. When I turned five years old, my parents began sending me by myself. I would fly unaccompanied, and they would drive down to meet me two or three weeks later. It was complicated travel; the airlines had names that aligned with a compass: Northwest out of Minneapolis to Atlanta, then a flight on Southern Airways for the last leg to Birmingham. While the bombings and racial tumult at the time may have prevented us from going to certain parts of town, the chaos could not keep us away from Birmingham.

"You got off the train. You went to the black neighborhoods and you kept your butt in the black neighborhoods until it was time to go home," my mother said. Whenever we ventured downtown, we'd always map out a route so that we'd know exactly where to find colored restrooms in case someone couldn't hold their water. And when we visited relatives in the country, there was always a coffee can in the trunk.

Until recently, I never understood how much of Alabama lives in me. I always identify myself as Minnesotan. But the spirit of Ensley resides in my soul. The rock-solid sense of community. The way everyone on the street claimed you as their own. The safe harbor on every porch along the block. Neighbors who went out of their way to talk to each other every day, saying, "C'mon up here, girl, and have a cool drink" or "Why don't you sit down and snap some peas with me?" or "I got the Braves game on the radio, want to sit for a spell?"

I sensed more communal love raining down on me in Ensley than at any other time in my life. Maybe it was a childhood illusion, but back in Alabama, I felt as if everywhere you turned someone cheered you on—and not just family members. Everybody was in the same boat, rowing in the same direction, determined to get somewhere better fast.

The irony is that when so many of us got there, the community bonds began to fray. A generation that had championed pioneers—the first professional black baseball player, the first black Supreme Court justice, the first black city council member, the first black this or that—knew all too well, in the early days of integration, that only a chosen few would get to the top.

As universities and law firms tiptoed toward diversity, only a handful of slots would be available to blacks. So parents who'd publicly championed black progress in general would secretly kneel in prayer at night, begging the Lord to let their children be among the lucky few. "Let opportunities rain on all our children, but please, Lord, if they're only taking one at the law or medical school, or just one in the National Honor Society or at the recital, please, Lord, let it be my baby."

Ensley was cocoonlike, and I would have spent almost all my time in the neighborhood if not for my grandfather. After he retired, he deputized me to join him on his daily errands. Grandpa was a huge man. Very tall. Very dark. Very proud. A former steelworker who wore suits every day after he stopped working at the mill, he'd tell us, "Dress for where you're going." I'm not sure he ever got there, but I guess his dark suit and skinny tie signaled where his grandkids were headed.

He drove a big car. Really big. Shiny and dark, with doors that opened at the middle of each side—suicide doors, as they were called. They made it easier to load people and cargo. This was important, because Grandpa rode "jitney." You see, few people had sedans in Ensley then. My grandfather, a lifelong saver, had waited until he could buy a very big car with cash, not simply for enjoyment but to help him earn money during his retirement. He drove people to and from the grocery store or the doctor or wherever they had to go. This was called riding jitney.

During my summer stays in Birmingham, my grandfather usually carried me into town with him on trips to Bruno's, the big grocery store. I would have to get dressed up for the day in a starchy little pinafore and patent leather shoes. And since this was before the days of car seats, I would sit next to him in the massive front seat, the two of us in what most people would call Sunday-go-to-meeting clothes. Some days, when we parked the car and walked into the business district, my grandfather would be approached by men in work uniforms. They lived in a section across a creek that I later learned was home to Irish and Italian families. They always looked rumpled. They had dirt on their faces, and their hair always seemed wet. They called my grandfather "boy" and "nigrah," which was supposed to be slightly less offensive and confrontational than *nigger.* Slightly.

Sometimes they'd ask him who he "thought" he was, driving a big car and dressing like a preacher. They would follow us, barking and sneering and spitting on the sidewalk. They would step in front of us now and then to block our way. My grandfather said little. He knew the men by name. I remember that he would sometimes tell them to give his regards to their parents or ask after someone he used to work with at the mills. This would often get the men to back off, allowing us to continue on our way—a man with hands the size of mitts holding on to an overdressed child.

I now wonder whether the little girl in the lace socks and patent leather shoes was invited along for the ride to provide Grandpa with a measure of protection from Birmingham hostility. I can't imagine putting my own kids into a similar situation, dressing them up as armor for their grandparents. I ran this by Mom, wanting her to say, "You're crazy" or "Your imagination is running away with you." But instead she allowed, "We lived in different times. People did what they had to do." To get by, people had to rely on their wits and control their emotions.

My father used to joke that he and his five brothers, both in looks and temperament, seemed to fall in line with Snow White's seven dwarfs, except Dopey. "There are no dumb folks in my household," my grandfather used to say. If you spent any time at all in the little wooden bungalow on Avenue G you would have heard Belvin Norris Sr. assert as much time and again, as if praying or making a promise. He might say it proudly, or spit it out like a stern warning to underscore a command, as in: "Boy, you better figure out how to fix that broken faucet so the eight people in this house can get washed in time for church." Silence, then: "I may not know much, but I know one thing. There are no dumb folks in my household." Grandpa Belvin repeated this so often that, if the little Birmingham bungalow had housed a business, the sign out front most likely would have read, GREAT FOOD. GOOD PEOPLE. NO DUMMIES.

As I grew older I began to understand my dad's joke about the seven dwarfs. Dopey aside, the personalities of these six black sons of Birmingham seemed to correspond to those of Snow White's little friends. Sylvester, the oldest, would be Sneezy. He was the eccentric, always dabbing at his face with a white hanky as he sketched out music and poetry in a little notebook. Louis would be Sleepy, though all his brothers called him Nip, even though they knew it was a derogatory term, because the deep slant of his eyes made him look slightly Asian. Simpson was Grumpy because he often was grumpy. He was hot-tempered, hardworking, and tightly wound. When he laughed, only his eyes would smile. His chin remained tight—the sign of a man who never let his guard down; though he could be an absolute softie around kids. In contrast, Woodrow had an impish grin all his life, even when his skin wrinkled and his hair turned gray. The name Bashful suits him best. Doc? That would be Joe Nathan, the youngest and smartest of the bunch, who never let you forget it. My father, Belvin, would naturally be Happy, for his perennially upbeat disposition.

Until the end of his life, Dad was an infernally cheerful man, always smiling, always trying to make others feel at ease. I am now ashamed to say that there were times when his demeanor made me uneasy, moments when he would smile at, and joke with, salespeople or waitresses who had shown disdain or disrespect. His manner may have suited him well for his job as a window clerk at the post office, but to a kid raised in the sock-it-to-me seventies, his penchant to please struck me as submissive. Only here's the thing: years later, I now see the same trait in myself, and it no longer makes me cringe in quite the same way, for I now understand that his aversion to conflict and his compulsive need for calm are what got us through the roughest patches in our lives. What I did not understand until recently is that it also got him through his own darkest days.

6

A Secret

I HAVE COME TO THE CONCLUSION that when people start a sentence with "You know," they're trying to take the edge off unsettling news. Think about it. All those times you've heard "You know, I hate to tell you this" or "You know, this relationship has not been working out." Or even "You know, I love you." "You know" suggests a seed of doubt; maybe you don't really know, after all. I was certainly in the dark when Uncle Joe surprised me over breakfast one morning a few years ago. Joe Nathan Norris is my father's only surviving brother. He was supposed to be called Jonathan, but someone got it wrong on his birth certificate. These days he likes to call himself "the Last of the Mohicans" or "the Last Man Standing"—dignified titles that hint at the loneliness of a man who has too quickly run out of brothers to call when he needs advice or has news he wants to share.

At breakfast that morning Uncle Joe blurted out a secret: "You know, your father was shot." Six shattering words uttered in a matter-of-fact way before Joe shoved a spoonful of oatmeal into his mouth. "Shot in the leg," he continued, churning the spoon in the bowl full of gruel, as if constant motion would enhance the flavor. I have always been close to Joe. When I was a kid, he rewarded my love of books with a steady stream of suggested reading, and now we have a special bond because I was the only one in our big, loud family who could huddle with him in a corner and talk about the jazz musician Jaco Pastorius or the Argentine dissident Jacobo Timerman.

My work frequently takes me to Chicago, and whenever I blow through town, I swing by to see my uncle on the Far South Side, in Pill Hill, so named because many black doctors once lived there. On this particular trip, though, my schedule was tight, and so that Thursday morning Joe drove to meet me downtown at the West Egg Cafe, an all-day breakfast spot near the Lake Michigan waterfront that's popular with yuppies. He had ordered his oatmeal and I some Tex-Mex egg concoction, even as Joe made a point of reminding me that for the price of a piece of toast we could have both enjoyed a whole spread at any one of a dozen joints on the South Side. No sense in arguing. He was right, though his protest was a bit hollow.

In truth, Joe didn't mind heading downtown to break his routine. He had become the primary caretaker for my aunt Odiev, whose kidney disease required frequent dialysis, and he also doted on a firstborn granddaughter with cerebral palsy. In other words, he spent his retirement earning his sainthood and he never complained. He also needed to stop downtown at the Obama campaign office to pick up some yard signs and flyers. Like so many older black Americans, Joe felt that the hope Obama offered was much more than just a four-letter word.

Uncle Joe's news about my dad's shooting was tangential; he went on a rant about a completely different subject, grousing about black men and black leadership and why so many black people had given up hope, even though their lives were so much easier than their forebears' had been. Joe had the heart of an activist. He'd left a comfortable teaching job in Hyde Park to start a pilot project working with juvenile inmates in the Cook County Jail, kids whose rap sheets were so treacherous that they were tried and remanded as adults. The assignment would be hell on earth for most people, but Joe saw an opportunity to reach a captive audience; his pupils couldn't skip class or threaten the teacher without inviting a beat-down by prison guards. He introduced his students to works by Paul

Laurence Dunbar, James Baldwin, Richard Wright, Ralph Ellison, Ernest Gaines, Chester Himes, and even Chinua Achebe and Mark Mathabane. When he knew he had won their trust, he made them read Rudolph Fisher's *The Walls of Jericho,* the better to understand an important life lesson: that a man is truly tough only when he can show his soft side. He turned criminals into readers, and in exchange he asked for only one thing: that they continue to read upon release from jail.

His years with the Cook County cons had left Joe with some hard theories about young black men. "They have it too easy. They don't know what struggle is. They always want to blame somebody else. They want a handout. They don't take care of business." If you didn't interrupt him, he might go on for hours. Get an older black man riled up about today's young folk and his vitriol might outdo that of even the most outrageous conservative commentator. At our Thursday breakfast, Joe was worked up. He'd asked the juvies which leaders they looked up to; they had rattled off the names of rappers and athletes. No surprise there. When he'd clarified that he was asking about elected officials, they'd cracked up and all but told him to go to hell. Politics, they'd said, is for white folks. So Joe was on a rant, upset at the juvies for throwing their lives away, upset at black leaders who couldn't figure out how to inspire young people, upset that he had to work so hard as a precinct captain to get young black folk to vote. Even his own son was unregistered. "Don't they know what people had to do to give them the right to vote?" he asked.

Joe continued, on a roll, before dropping the bomb: "You know, your father was shot." He must have seen the look on my face, the confusion in my eyes, the utter shock. In a world of my own, I heard the tap-tap of his spoon against the ceramic bowl. He pushed his breakfast aside and took a slow deep breath before puffing out his cheeks as if to suppress a belch, the kind of thing older men do all the time; but since I interview people for a living, I know this can also be a stalling tactic to take the measure of things. Uncle Joe had never been one to pussyfoot through uncomfortable conversations. When I was a kid, he'd had an outsized reputation for telling it like it was. If your legs were ashen, he'd be the first to say you forgot to use lotion, loud enough for everyone in church to hear. If an adult got up without taking his plate to the sink, well, they'd hear about that, too. If we were going to the movies on a Saturday afternoon and there were six cousins on hand and only four seats in the sedan, Joe Norris would just cut to the chase: "Two of y'all won't be seeing a movie today. I don't know which two, but whoever it is I don't want to see any tears. You kids got too much to be crying about anything."

But Uncle Joe had ceased being the family hard-ass long ago, and his weary grin indicated that he took no pleasure in bearing bad news. "Mickey," he said, reverting to my childhood nickname, "here's what I know." His anger about the juvies had melted, and though his voice could usually rattle the fish in Lake Michigan, his words were now slow and gentle. I had to lean in to hear his rasp. He didn't so much tell a story as deliver a series of statements. "They were down somewhere near Fourth Avenue trying to get onto an elevator. . . . Woody was pushed. . . . Belvin intervened. . . . A cop pulled out his gun. . . . Woody swatted at the cop's arm and the gun deflected downward. . . . In the end, Belvin was shot in the leg. . . . That's what I know." There was a lot to digest that morning in the restaurant, and none of it went down easily. Shot in the leg. By a cop. And in Jim Crow Alabama, to boot.

I was furious. Confused. My head hurt, and I wanted to scream. I needed details. Why did the cop push Uncle Woody? Where were they going? How serious was the injury? I peppered Uncle Joe with questions, careful not to show the anger welling up inside me. It felt like the room was starting to spin. Acid rose in my throat, and the Tex-Mex egg dish felt like a terrible choice. I swallowed hard, trying to repress the one question I really wanted to ask: "Why am I only hearing about this now?"

I was intent on gathering as many facts as I could before the waitress dropped the check, fearful that a window of opportunity might close. What if Uncle Joe's revelation had been only a moment of senior disinhibition? I knew not to seem too shocked or upset because then he might hold back, sensitive to my emotional fragility. As the youngest of six brothers, he'd been the last to enter the military and the last to return to Birmingham after the war. So he hadn't been there when the incident with my dad occurred. Perhaps for that reason, or because so many years had intervened, his facts were fuzzy, his story sparse. He had always been the most confident among the Norris clan, but this morning he appeared outside his comfort zone. As we talked about Alabama policemen, I spied a vestige of fear on the face of a man who worked with convicts every day, and who earned their respect by showing that he could do more than just talk about putting a foot up their behinds.

Yet, this normally confident man was clearly disturbed by a hazy memory from more than sixty years ago. "The only reason they were not killed on the spot is because of the crowd," he said. "If they were on a road or in an alley, they'd be gone." With that he stretched his neck, looked away, and sighed. "We can talk more later," he offered in closing. I couldn't ignore what he'd told me. I phoned him time and again over the next few weeks, and in each conversation he seemed to regret having said the little he had; the details he offered were few, if not speculative.

Apparently, it had happened in Birmingham somewhere around Fourth Avenue—the black business corridor. My father was still in his twenties and had just returned from service in the navy during World War II. He was not alone. My uncle Woody was with him and maybe one or two other friends.

There was a charge of resisting arrest, and the family had just wanted the episode to go away. "Knowing your father," Joe explained, "he would have wanted to downplay it. My mother would have wanted to be more aggressive, but it takes money and power to be aggressive. We had neither."

"Shot in the leg." "Belvin was shot in the leg." Every time I hear these words in my mind, I think of the ever so slight lilt in my father's step, so minor you might miss it if you weren't paying close attention, so subtle that I thought it was an affectation, the way some black men put a little music in their walk. Daddy had always had a distinctive gait. Come to think of it, all his brothers did, to varying degrees. Black folk call it putting a little English in your walk, using a pool hall term for something special or unique. When I learned of the injury, I realized that his gait might have been born of pain, not pride. But Joe's account made no sense. My dad in a violent encounter with the police? It just did not compute.

How could a man who always observed stop signs, a man who always filed his taxes early and preached that jaywalking proved a weakness of character have been involved in an altercation with Alabama policemen? Why would he hide it from his children? Why would he impart life lessons to us about looking the other way, turning the other cheek, respecting those who lived across the color line in spite of insults hurled our way, when he himself had not?

I always knew that my father had had his mysteries, like the FBI Wanted poster for Angela Davis that I found inside his dresser drawer after he died. Or the way he would slip out of the house on Thursday nights, after he and my mother got divorced, to meet a date I was not supposed to know about. Or that odd encounter in the upstairs bathroom, when he walked in and asked if he could borrow my Afro pick, the thick, black plastic one with a handle shaped like a clenched fist. For a time, he slipped it into his back pocket, the Black Power fist peeking from his slacks. To me, the Alabama incident shed new light on this.

My father loved music, yet there were certain types he could not tolerate. I went to high school at a time when seventies southern rock was all over the airwaves. Acts such as the Charlie Daniels Band, the Allman Brothers Band, and Lynyrd Skynyrd topped the charts with songs like "Free Bird" and "The South's Gonna Do It Again." Dad could stomach almost any kind of music we brought home: funk, metal, folk, even punk. But he had little patience for southern rock, the kind of music good ole boys would blare from the backs of pickup trucks outfitted with gun racks and Confederate flags.

One rock anthem in particular pushed him past the edge: "Sweet Home Alabama." I remember one morning when I was loudly accompanying the song on the radio while fiddling with my curling iron. The group Lynyrd Skynyrd was singing about Birmingham and how much they loved the "guv-ner." The song referred to Governor George Wallace, who blocked school integration despite JFK's orders. It was more than he could bear. He leaned into my bedroom, gritting his teeth, and shouted, "Turn that trash off now!" My father was a quiet man, thoughtful, funny, bookish. He loved to listen to jazz and read the Sunday *New York Times.* He rarely raised his voice and spoke with profound economy when he said anything at all. You could say he was very Zen. Loud talk or power-to-the-people defiance was not his style, though he must have had some steel in his spine to leave Alabama, head north, and use the G.I. Bill to become a block buster on the South Side of Minneapolis.

He had to have had some grit to secure a mortgage and move his family to the far South Side, on Oakland Avenue, where all the lawns were green and all the families white. He had to have had fortitude to endure a bullet wound, even a minor one. All the same, the incident must have battered his dignity, while setting an internal compass that allowed him to move forward and shut out anything that might refresh that painful memory. His leg may have been injured, but his pride was intact.

I'm reminded of a film I watched time and again in high school, *Monty Python and the Holy Grail.* In one hilarious scene, a character called the Black Knight is stuck in mud, outmatched and wounded, yet still keeps mouthing off at his enemy. His arms and legs have been severed. Blood is spurting from his wounds. He's a wreck, but in his jaunty English accent he insists that he's invincible.

"Merely a flesh wound," he chirps.

"I want to meet the man who shot my father." Even as I said this to myself over and over, nothing about the sentence felt right. This is the kind of thing gangsters or gunslingers say, not middle-aged women from Minneapolis whose parents trudged off to work at the post office. Yet the desire to confront my father's shooter became an obsession, and then an ache. I hectored my relatives and some of my father's high school classmates to tell me what they knew; I was astonished when some acknowledged that they'd heard about the shooting yet brushed aside my questions with utter nonchalance. One of my father's cousins was so rattled by my importunity that he fussed at me as if I were still a six-year-old. "Girl, stop pestering me about details," he said. "Stuff like that used to happen, but we never really dwelled on it. We moved on, and so should you." He was wasting his breath. There was no going back for me. I needed answers.

But the details of the shooting grew more vague with each telling. Dad was alone with Woody. No, wait, that's not how my third cousin in Alabama remembered it. He was certain Dad was with a group of young men. Some of his high school classmates believed that a white woman was involved and that my dad failed to step aside fast enough when she passed. However, this account was roundly dismissed by relatives still living in Birmingham.

Though Dad never told me or Mom or my sisters about the episode, some of his brothers had apparently talked to their children about it. My first cousin Butch had known for years. He'd heard about it from his father during a cautionary "never look a cop in the eye" conversation, the kind black men often have with their teenage sons. Butch irrefutably dismissed the story about the white woman: "If a white woman was involved, your father would have been dead."

For months, I could not find anybody willing to talk at length about the incident. At some point he or she would shut down, sometimes with pleasantries or stern warnings not to bring the matter up again. My father's cousin Edgar Carr suggested that amnesia was a coping skill. "If they told you to forget it, you forgot about it. In fact, you forgot about it before they were finished talking." When I called my eighty-nine-year-old aunt Blanche, in Ohio, the music drained out of her voice as soon as I brought the subject up. "So now you know," she said. I could picture her holding the phone, shaking her head, and looking down at her slippers. "A man can't talk about a thing like that. I think it took his life in the end. He never got over it. I think that is what killed him. He never got over it. He lived his whole life with fear in his heart." Her advice to me before hanging up the phone was "Don't let this make you bitter. You have so much in life."

Two weeks later a letter came in the mail. "Despite all I said, I want you to [know] your father was very happy in his life and he was very proud of you," Aunt Blanche had written. "We do our best to do right by our children. Try to understand."

7

The Docket

I'D BEEN IN BIRMINGHAM only a few times after high school, mostly to chase down stories as a professional reporter. Truly to understand my father's experience, I had to travel back to Alabama. I had little to go on. No date of the shooting; no location; no names other than Woody's and my father's. I didn't know whether Dad had been alone or with others, or whether the police or sheriff's department had been involved. So it's easy to understand why Jim Baggett was polite but guarded when I called to tell him I desperately needed his help. Jim heads the Department of Archives and Manuscripts at the Birmingham Public Library, and while he listened patiently to my ramblings on the phone, he must have thought I was just this side of crazy.

Patient and kind, with a slightly caustic wit, Jim was careful not to douse my hopes. He explained that it would be "pert near" impossible to find a record of so obscure an occurrence. He added that incidents like my father's shooting had been "fairly common."

"The Birmingham police shot a lot of people," he said. "The city was like a shooting gallery back then." Birmingham police records from the era are scarce, and Jim warned me repeatedly that arrest records, especially those from the post–World War II era, were unavailable, consigned to oblivion. Birmingham police archives are notoriously hard to track down. The few files that survive have been pored over by lawyers and countless civil rights researchers. Or they've been pillaged by those seeking to profit from or plunder souvenirs. I learned, for instance, that most mug shots of the young demonstrators arrested at the children's marches during the peak of the civil rights standoff, in the spring of 1963, are missing. So, too, are the rosters of the police officers on duty on those days. Documents so important to this country's modern history have simply vanished.

This meant that tracking down the precise details of my father's case would be difficult, maybe even impossible. "The only way you're likely to find anything," Jim told me, "is if it made the papers, and it would have to be the black papers because the white newspapers would never ever print a story like this. They just didn't care." On the phone seven hundred miles away, Baggett, I knew, could tell I'd been stung by his statement. "Let me see what I can do," he offered, cautioning once again that unearthing even a scintilla of information about my father's shooting would be like finding the proverbial needle in a haystack. "But every so often," he said, "someone sits down and lands right smack on top of it, so let's see what we find." It was all I could ask for. I felt in my bones that there was something out there waiting to be found.

In the meantime, I swam in a sea of what-ifs. What if my father had tried in his own way to tell me about the shooting but, with the callowness of youth, I had signaled that I couldn't be bothered? What if the officer who had shot him was still alive? What exactly was I going to say when I showed up at his doorstep or, more likely, confronted him in his bathrobe in a nursing home? What if he didn't remember the incident after all these years? What if he told me, "Yeah, I did it—your father was a real jackass"? What if I got arrested myself for smacking an old white man upside the head? I was losing it. What if the bullet had not grazed my father's leg but had caused far greater harm? What if he had bled to death? What if he had been crippled? One night, I looked around the kitchen at my husband and my kids and their crayon drawings all over the place and thought: None of this would even exist if the trajectory of the bullet had been different. My fate had been a matter of serendipity.

On the evening of July 7, 2009, the fog of my imaginings began to clear. My husband, Broderick Johnson, was in California on business and I had just had dinner with my kids. As I'd watched them slurp long spaghetti strands and dissolve into fits of giggling, I'd resisted the urge to fuss. How could I when they looked so adorable? I watched over the brushing of their teeth, and we all climbed into my daughter's twin bed to read a wonderful children's classic, *The Hundred Dresses,* a book about the moral dilemma of childhood teasing. Are you just as guilty if you sit back and say nothing while a child mercilessly teases another? The object of the taunts in the book is a poor little Polish girl named Wanda Petronski, and given the book's publication date of 1944, it's clear that the parable about having the courage to stand up for what's right alluded to the plight of persecuted Jews in Europe. During our reading, it could have been taken as the oppression of marginalized "Negroes" in the United States. The simple eloquence of children's literature can sometimes shoot straight to the heart.

With my two young children drifting off, I headed back to the kitchen to load the dishwasher and scrub pots and pans. I heard a ping in my purse, my iPhone telling me, "You've got mail." I rinsed my hands to have a look, thinking that Broderick had left me a voice mail while I was upstairs reading to the kids. It was, instead, an email from Birmingham; the subject line: "Your Father." "Michele, . . . found that Belvin and Woodrow Norris were arrested February 7, 1946, for drunkenness, robbery and resisting arrest. They were convicted of drunkenness and resisting arrest the following day in recorders court. . . . found the info in jail and court dockets. There you go. Talk soon."

Drunkenness, robbery, resisting arrest? The ugly charges

couldn't be true, I thought. My dad had never been one to hit the sauce hard. Had he lived it up with some navy buddies that night only to suffer the consequences? As for robbery, that, too, had to be wrong. It just had to be. For weeks I had been tracking down information in the manner of a journalist, though I'd wondered whether the story had substance, whether it might be nothing but family legend. I'd been besieged by hearsay. No one I'd spoken to had actually been with my father when the shooting happened; no one could prove anything, even that it had happened. But the email message erased that doubt. My father's name was in a jail docket and court records.

His story, or at least a police officer's version of it, had been written down in pencil and ink. My knees buckled; I collapsed to the floor and stayed there for nearly two hours. Everything I'd thought I knew about my father had been turned inside out. I was in a bind. I had to go to Alabama. But first I had to throw up.

During my childhood and adolescence, Alabama had been a second home to me. I spent weeks there each summer visiting my grandparents, absorbing the city's rhythms and social codes. I could slip in and out of the loose-voweled Alabama accent as easily as pulling a sock on. But when I returned to Birmingham in search of my father's story, the familiar accent hit me like an odor as soon as I stepped off the plane.

Suspicion. That's what it was. The newspaper vendor in the gift shop. The woman behind the rental-car counter. The police officer directing traffic. Questions raced through my mind. On which side had these white people stood in Alabama's race war? Were they related somehow to strict enforcers of the Jim Crow laws of yore? Had their kinfolk spat on schoolchildren or turned dogs and water cannons on civil rights protesters? Were any related to the policeman who shot my father?

I knew the score in Alabama. I understood that the state had more than its share of people who wanted to keep black folks in their place, although I had been schooled to look past that. But now my blinders had fallen off: the man who had preached to me to look the other way may have purposefully kept from me a defining racial confrontation in his life.

By the time I arrived in Alabama I had compiled a few more facts about my father's "incident." I knew that the day he'd been arrested, February 7, 1946, had been a Thursday. And I had learned that meeting the man who shot my father would be far more difficult than I'd imagined. The story was not simple; more than one officer had been involved. Clues to what happened that night had long been locked away in the bowels of the Birmingham Public Library's Linn-Henley Research Library, a beautiful neoclassical building with large windows and thick majestic columns. That building had been off-limits to me as a child. Although the library officially integrated in 1963, it would be years before my grandparents would allow us to set foot in it.

In Ensley, my grandparents had joined forces with cash-strapped neighbors to form their own library lending system. No two families ever purchased the same book, except for the trinity of books that graced every working-class home. Every family had at least one Bible and often a special one, with the family tree drawn on the back. Most families also had another book nearly as important: a little dog-eared paperback dream book offering guidance for playing the numbers. And among families with school-aged children, small dictionaries were common. Books were sold door-to-door to black families at special discounts, and inspirational messages stamped inside told about the fruits of hard work and the power of industry.

The Ensley neighbors devised a collective purchasing plan. If one family bought an atlas, that was checked off the master list. The same held true if another household purchased a thesaurus, a large dictionary, or one of the volumes in the *Treasury of the Familiar* short-story collection. Even the encyclopedia was purchased on a neighborhood-wide installment plan. One family would spring for the first two *Britannica* volumes, another would buy the next two, and so on until the set was complete.

So it was that the 900 block of Avenue G had acquired its own reference library. The books were displayed on high shelves in living rooms or locked away until needed in a wooden chifforobe. Who had read what and when was carefully etched in each volume. Often the adults who purchased the books barely understood the words contained within. But they derived great joy from propping their feet on the porch railing and listening to their children read aloud from the encyclopedia or a dictionary in the cool of evening.

This is what I was thinking about when I walked through the turnstile of the Linn-Henley building, past the reading room, with its amazingly ornate Ezra Winter murals, and down to the basement archives, where Jim Baggett presides over the special collection of Alabama history.

Jim is a researcher's dream, smart and thorough and slightly obsessed with the small details that give a story weight and drama. And what a storyteller! Libraries were fixed in my mind as places where conversation was kept to a minimum and, if necessary, was whispered apologetically. That's mostly true at the Birmingham Public Library. But Jim oversees his own little fiefdom, tucked under a marble staircase and closed off by a glass door. It's a space where stories are kept and told with brio, in painterly detail, and accompanied by laughter.

The laughter threw me for a loop at first. Jim knows Birmingham inside out. He's proud of his city, and he makes no apologies for its "unfortunate chapters." He also does not defend Alabama's segregationists. When he told his stories, there was no shame or hyperbole, and he managed to find humor even where, as I saw it, there was none. Imagine Burl Ives relating the most dramatic and painful chapters of Alabama's history. You are entertained even when you want to look away. He is a steady and fair steward of the city's troubled history. Jim directed me to two massive leather-bound dockets, one from the court and one from the city's main jail. They were well worn and big enough to cover a library display table. I spent hours poring over dusty pages smelling of mold; as a result, I caught a nasty sinus infection.

Baggett first guided me to the warden's docket for the Southside Prison. In it I found a rogue's catalog of men arrested and charged with all manner of offenses, organized in neat columns, like the ledger my father had used to document household expenses. Each handwritten entry detailed the facts of an arrest: date, time, type of offense, names of the prisoner and of the arresting officers. There were handwriting styles galore, suggesting varying degrees of education and even pride in penmanship.

February 7, 1946, appears to have been a busy night at the jail. Fifteen men were arrested within a three-hour period, a few for robbery, one for assault with a weapon. Most, however, were charged with drunkenness or vagrancy. You snap to attention when you see your own name in writing, much as you do when you hear someone say it aloud. I was prepared to see Norris in the docket, yet still I grew tense when my eyes fell on it. Prisoner number 7562, a twenty-two-year-old black male, arrested at 9:50 p.m. by two officers named Lindsey and Espy. The name of the man arrested: Woodrow Norris.

An hour or so later another Norris was booked. My father, Belvin Norris Jr., a twenty-year-old black male. He was signed in at 10:45 p.m. by three arresting officers. Lindsey and Espy again, and another named Pate. Nothing suggested which officer had shot my father. In fact, there was no mention of a gunshot wound at all.

I was struck by the hour lag between the arrest of my uncle Woodrow and that of my dad. What had happened? Had my father been treated for his injury before being booked? Since my father had supposedly intervened when Woody was pushed by a cop, did the cops take him somewhere to teach him a lesson? Was he in pain when they threw him into the jail cell? I have spent hours staring at these docket entries, trying to piece together the story they tell—obviously a complex one that had unfolded as the evening wore on.

It appears that the Norris men were first arrested for robbery, the charge ascribed in the docket to both men, the word written in separate hands and different ink—blue and black. Someone else had scribbled "drunk" under each name, again in different handwriting and ink. On a third line appeared "resisting arrest" under each name, the handwriting suggesting yet another officer. I would later discover upon reviewing the records for my father's court appearance that there was a total of five arresting officers: Lindsey, Espy, Pate, and two others named Neil and Baggett. Despite coincidence, the officer Baggett has no relation to the Birmingham archivist Jim Baggett, who helped lead me to this discovery.

I noticed something else while examining the warden's docket—or, I should say, someone else. Below Woodrow's entry was one for John Beaton, a twenty-one-year-old black male from 904 Avenue G, two doors down from the Norris house. He was signed in at 9:40 p.m., ten minutes before Woodrow. The Beaton and Norris families were close, and John had attended Parker High with Woody and Belvin. The docket showed that John Beaton had also been charged with robbery, the word "drunk" also added to his record after he was booked. That was all. Beaton was not charged with resisting arrest.

John Beaton gave me another path to pursue. Woody and Belvin had taken the story of what happened that night to their graves. Woody kept it to himself, and my father never said a word to his family about the night he had spent in a Birmingham jail. But if John Beaton or other Beatons were alive, I might have another avenue to pursue.

The Norris brothers appear to have had no cash when arrested, but Beaton had sixteen dollars on him. Woody's prisoner effects were an overcoat and a fedora. "Disc. Papers" appeared under my father's name. The term didn't click with me at first, but eventually I figured out what it meant: military discharge papers. Belvin Norris's service in the navy, it appeared, had recently ended, for he was still carrying his papers around. His welcome home had been perplexing, in light of the events on February 7, 1946. He escaped the war without injury. He wasn't so fortunate when he returned home.

8

Service

YEARS IN THE MILITARY HAD MARKED the men ruling the households in our neighborhood in Minnesota. Every time you stepped into someone's living room, a distinguished man in uniform stared back at you. No matter how jowly or bald my schoolmates' fathers were in middle age, the military portraits proudly placed on mantels and dining room buffets preserved their chiseled youth. Men fighting a sedentary lifestyle's battle of the bulge would loosen their trousers and settle into their recliners to throw back a cold beer while watching the evening news or chuckling along with Johnny Carson. Every so often, when the daily grind would cease, they would gaze upon the old picture of a younger man looking past the camera, into the middle distance. Whether smiling or serious, their confident expression seemed to say, "We saved the world and we know it."

These World War II veterans didn't need Tom Brokaw to tell them that theirs was the greatest generation. They had only to look at those vintage eight-by-tens to feel a shimmer of pride and gratitude. Perhaps they also felt a thud in their gut, remembering the berserk scrum of war. Now the boys in the photos were working-class men who had learned to compartmentalize their feelings with grim efficiency—a common survival tactic after climbing out of foxholes or submarines. Tending the nest is often women's work, but I suspect it was the men who took it upon themselves to display their wartime portraits. They were the ones who nailed the hooks in the wall or created altarlike arrangements of their photographs and service medals.

I remember visiting one of my father's best friends, a fellow postal worker named George Newcombe. I loved going to the Newcombe house. Everything there was slightly exotic. Mrs. Newcombe was from the Ukraine, and her accent was as delightful as the sweet and sticky noodle kugels she churned out. The Newcombes had a bunch of rowdy kids who were all wicked smart. An afternoon at their home felt like a marathon session of the game show *Jeopardy!* because the kids were always involved in some sort of smarty-pants one-upmanship.

"Name all the capitals of all the states that start with the letter *M*."

"Quick—Henry the Eighth had six wives. Name them—in order!"

"What's the difference between Euclidean geometry and Riemannian geometry?"

"Who's the voice of Foghorn Leghorn?"

Dad liked to retreat to the relative quiet of the basement and ogle the latest addition to Mr. Newcombe's impossibly elaborate train set. If you know anyone who has kept a train set, you can fix a picture in your mind. If you've never seen the work of a model-train obsessive, then imagine the layout of a miniature Norman Rockwell town, with dime stores, pie shops, and kids carrying books tied together with leather straps, a town that fits on a dining room table. Mr. Newcombe's town sat on a ten-by-twelve-foot raised platform, slightly higher than a big dining room table. In that compact little metropolis, the excruciatingly detailed buildings were all about six inches tall. The trees "growing" out of the Astroturf even changed colors according to the seasons. A neon sign glowed outside the diner. The pole at the barbershop rotated. Fireplaces glowed in the houses along Main Street. A tiny train snaked through the elevated hamlet—over hills, through tunnels, and across pastures of Astroturf, blowing its whistle and belching little puffs of smoke.

In the seventies, the South Side of Minneapolis was filled with train enthusiasts. They were always men who would meticulously transform their basements into hideaways, where they exercised complete control over a noisy little world of their own making. Perhaps that was the draw for working-class men whose lives revolved around forty-hour workweeks, thirty-day mortgage cycles, and fierce Minnesota cold fronts swooping in without warning.

When George and my dad finally emerged from what we would now call "the man cave," my father would yell upstairs, "Hey, squirt, get your stuff together, it's time to get on home." We always said our good-byes in the Newcombes' formal living room, with its overlay lace curtains and replica oil lamps, a parlor that recalled the world of *Doctor Zhivago.* Mr. Newcombe would usually display a tic as we were leaving. I'm not sure that he was even aware of it. Walking us toward the door, he would pass by a low, long table where his army photo sat. His hands would slip out of his pockets for just a second. He would pause just long enough to reach out and slightly adjust the crystal frame, the way a mother, without thinking, might reach out to brush a stray eyelash off her young one's cheek. In one small gesture, an involuntary surge of love, pride, and vulnerability. An essential part of his manhood was trapped in that frame.

My father's military service had always been a bit of a mystery. I had no idea how the experience had shaped him. He never spoke much about it, and although we had many pictures displayed in our home, there were none from his stint in the navy. His military photos were shoved in a box buried in a basement closet where we stored the Christmas ornaments. His service medal was hidden in a back corner of a bureau drawer, beneath a pile of letters and greeting cards, mostly from my sisters and me, drawn with crayons or adorned with tissue-paper rosettes. I discovered Dad's medal when I cleaned out his bedroom after he died.

But I was a child when I stumbled on the treasure trove of black-and-white vintage photos in the closet behind the basement stairs. Several showed Dad in a dark uniform. Sometimes he wore a white sailor's hat. Sometimes a black tam with U.S. NAVY embroidered on the band across his forehead. I forget what I was looking for in that dank space when I found the photos. As I held up the pictures under the naked closet light bulb, a kid, it seemed, was staring back at me. In every shot, Dad looked directly at the camera, the way nine-year-olds pose and wait to yell "Cheese!"

His grin was almost as wide as his sailor collar. His shoulders were so slim and his neck so twiggish that he resembled a boy who had just raided his big brother's closet to play Let's Pretend. To understand my father—a man I thought I knew so well—I had to understand the man-child in these pictures. I had to comprehend the journey he had taken to become the quiet man who taught me the most important lessons of my life.

On August 6, 1943, convulsions of war were felt around the globe. Near the Solomon Islands, six American destroyers intercepted and all but demolished a small Japanese fleet attempting to deliver troops and supplies to an enemy base at Kolombangara.[1] Also on that Friday, Italian government officials met with the German foreign minister to offer assurances that they would not negotiate a separate peace with the Allies. In Lithuania's Vilna ghetto, more than a dozen Jews were shot while attempting to resist deportation orders. In Berlin, nonessential residents were evacuated from the city.

On that day Belvin Norris Sr. proudly escorted his namesake to the navy recruiting station in room 25 of the Federal Building in Birmingham. Belvin Jr. was five days shy of his eighteenth birthday, so his father had to be on hand to sign the consent and declaration form for enlistment of a minor under eighteen.

That afternoon they had set out from a home that had grown much quieter in recent years. Sylvester, the oldest brother, was working as a Pullman porter, spending most of his time traveling all over the country by rail. Simpson and Louis had joined the army, leaving just three of the Norris boys on Avenue G. Soon there would be only two. Though his brothers were in the army, Belvin set his sights on the navy, perhaps because the navy had set its sights on men like him.

Though top leadership in the navy had long been opposed to the use of "Negroes in the Fleet," things were changing by 1943.[2] The navy was under tremendous pressure to loosen its policy. The pressure was coming from the White House, the War Manpower Commission, and even the army, whose commanding officers felt that their branch had accepted more than its share of black enlistees. It was also coming from surprising places. Elected officials from cities and towns throughout the South had expressed worries about population imbalance and social unrest: legions of able-bodied white men had marched off to war; most able-bodied blacks had stayed behind.

The chairman of the War Manpower Commission, Paul V. McNutt, echoed this concern in a memo to the secretary of the navy. "The low percentage of Negroes in the Army and in the Navy has resulted in a higher percentage of Negroes in the civilian population," McNutt wrote. "This condition has been the cause of continuous and mounting criticism. It poses grave implications . . . as the single white registrants disappear and husbands and fathers become the current white inductees, while single Negro registrants who are physically fit remain uninducted."[3] The message was clear: the combination of disproportionate numbers of single or unprotected white women and masses of single "physically fit" Negroes was cause for deep concern. Needless to say, this was not the only reason the navy shifted course.

By mid-1942, only a little more than 5,000 black men were serving in the navy, representing a mere 2 percent or so of the navy's male enlistees. Almost all were mess attendants or stewards. Now bowing to pressure, the navy, in January 1943, began admitting blacks to match their percentage of the total population. By February, black men in the navy amounted to 26,909; by the end of the year, more than 100,000 were on active duty.[4]

To reach its goals, the navy sought men with the right temperament, education, and maturity. A. H. Parker High, in Birmingham, was a natural place to look. Founded in 1899 as Birmingham's only high school for blacks, it was from its opening day held up as a citadel of excellence. With limited opportunities elsewhere, many of Birmingham's sharpest minds turned to teaching, so the Parker faculty resembled that of a small college. Nearly every instructor had a master's degree or a doctorate. Students from all over Alabama flocked to Parker, bunking with friends and relatives. Many walked miles to and from school every day. A. H. Parker High was so crowded that classes were in session both day and night, and graduation ceremonies were held in January and June.

With its rigorous academic program, no-nonsense discipline, and vocational classes in printing, mechanics, and nursing, Parker was the most reliable ticket to a better life for blacks in Birmingham. The school also had a storied college prep program. Universities across the country took notice, and so did the military. Newspapers at the time said Parker was the place to find men of character.

My father graduated from Parker in May 1943, and whatever ambitions he had were informed by the war raging across the ocean. Reminders of service and sacrifice were everywhere. Though he was on an accelerated-education track (taking physics, chemistry, and advanced math courses), college was beyond consideration. Money was tight. The nation was at war, so able-bodied men were expected to report for duty or to take an industrial job to aid wartime production.

Dad had grown up in the shadow of the steel mills and the blast of furnaces that made the night sky glow orange for hours before dawn, illuminating the little bungalows of relative prosperity along Avenue G. Birmingham still had its share of mill- and mineworkers who lived in shanties or company-owned tenements. But the simple houses in my family's neighborhood had a kind of aspirational charm, with curtained windows and proper outdoor furniture on the porch. If you stood at a corner and looked down Avenue G on an evening after the workday, you'd see cars parked in almost every driveway. To men and women whose parents or grandparents had been slaves, the stability must have afforded a peek of heaven.

Even so, Belvin senior wanted more for his sons. "There's a big ole world out there," he used to say. These simple words were meant to shoo his sons away from the backbreaking work in steel mills or coal mines and their occupational hazards, such as lost fingers and broken limbs, away from strikebreaker squabbles and black lung insurance claims. My grandfather's words were meant to encourage his sons to wander beyond a town where their station in life would always be defined by the color of their skin and where they could be killed for daring to question the status quo.

So if one's options were military service, work in the mills and mines, or other menial jobs, the choice was clear for high school graduate Belvin Norris Jr., who'd already spent three months sweeping and cleaning at the Phoenix office building downtown. A decision was reached: if Belvin junior had to wear a uniform, Belvin senior wanted it to be a military uniform.

When I tracked down Dad's service records I understood why he looked so young in his navy photos. At just over five foot eight, he weighed only 137 pounds. He had twenty-twenty vision and good blood pressure, and though he had suffered a bout of diphtheria as a kid, his health was deemed to be excellent. He enlisted for two years. At some point during the enlistment process someone had stamped his forms with the word "ruddy"—a term typically applied to dark-skinned whites. After his physical exam, the word was crossed out; "Negro" was typed to replace it. "Negro" was also stamped at least once, and often several times, on every document in his military file. "It is a unique art and special skill, this business of being a Negro in America," William H. Hastie, civilian aide to the secretary of war, was once moved to remark.

The year before Dad enlisted, the navy created a separate program for Negro recruits at Camp Robert Smalls, the naval station at Great Lakes, Illinois. Named in honor of a black Civil War hero, it had been established to prepare blacks for service beyond their conventional roles as stewards, mess attendants, and, occasionally, musicians. The camp was run by a white lieutenant commander, Daniel W. Armstrong, who was following family tradition. Commander Armstrong's father was a brigadier general who had led black troops in the Civil War and later founded Virginia's Hampton Institute, a historically black college whose alumni include Booker T. Washington. Armstrong held high hopes for the program, telling a *Time* magazine reporter in the first year of the war, "What we're doing here is bending every effort to make these boys as good as any fighting men the U.S. Navy has. The country doesn't yet know what a fine new source of fighting men the Navy has."[5]

Throughout the military, the majority of black men were

assigned to noncombat roles, building bridges, digging roads, collecting trash, shining shoes, driving trucks, and working on docks. Even those lucky enough to be promoted to metalsmith, mechanic, or gunner's mate received neither equal pay nor equal treatment. Decades after the war, historians would describe these men collectively as the physical backbone of the armed forces. Many of them had joined thinking that they were marching off to combat, or at least stepping closer to full citizenship. But, as they would come to learn, their service only confirmed their status as second-class Americans.

For my father, that cold realization came early. Three months after he arrived at Robert Smalls he was placed in the cooks and bakers program, and on November 9, 1943, he was transferred, along with thirty-nine other "Negro" recruits, to New Orleans for sixteen weeks of advanced kitchen training. The assignment meant that thereafter my father had to wear a small *C* on his upper sleeve, a rating badge denoting that his military service was all about serving others in the military. Fixing their meals. Baking their bread. Scrubbing pots. Washing dishes. All of this, while white men arriving at Great Lakes, regardless of skill or literacy, were automatically trained for work of a higher grade, as navy records indicate.

Over the course of my father's enlistment, the navy adopted new attitudes toward Negroes and their abilities, deciding that the marginalization of men with able bodies and agile minds only served to undermine the war effort. In February 1945, the navy published a new pamphlet for all naval officers; called the *Guide to Command of Negro Naval Personnel,* it spelled out the reversal of policy: "In modern total warfare any avoidable waste of manpower can only be viewed as material aid to the enemy. Restriction, because of racial theories, of the contribution of any individual to the war effort is a serious waste of human resources."[6]

My father's military file revealed a story he never spoke about, at least not to me. He wound up moving around quite a bit during his two and a half years in the navy. He was transferred to outposts in Pensacola and Williamsburg, San Francisco and Hawaii, and eventually to the supply division of the service support forces for the Pacific fleet, after, in March 1944, the navy decided that Negro cooks and bakers could assume new positions if whites were unavailable.[7] Dad received an honorable discharge from the navy in January 1946. He left service to his country with a hundred dollars in his pocket and the right to a World War II medal.

On those rare instances when Dad referred to his time in the navy, he was always breezy or humorous. At bedtime, he would march up the stairs like a soldier, trying to get the kids to follow him. Or he might hum military tunes while maneuvering his old-fashioned push mower. I can still see him striding up and down the lawn as he cut the grass, muttering, "Left, right, left, right, left!" He used to tell us that he learned to speed-peel potatoes and carrots on KP duty, boasting of his skill while making fun of our pathetic attempts to help Mom prepare supper.

My naïveté was laughable, as I'd imagined that just about everybody in the military had done KP duty, during initiation or as punishment. War movies I watched as a child on Saturday matinee television always showed men sweating over steaming cauldrons or washing mountains of dishes and silverware. I didn't realize at the time that a sink hose sprayer was the closest thing to a weapon many servicemen of color had been allowed to wield in World War II.

What must it have been like for a young man, barely eighteen years old, to discover that his country, fighting oppression overseas, was unashamed to marginalize him? In those days a young black man fully expected to encounter racism in the South. But an optimistic fellow would also have assumed that whites in the North were different, less prejudiced. Although the South could strangle your spirit, there was a bedrock belief that life would be easier up North, where the well-educated men who ran the country did not share in the fierce racial hatred consuming the offspring of the Confederacy. This optimistic young man might also have assumed that the collective wartime spirit would smooth over old divisions of race and class. But, as so many of these brown-skinned men came to realize, military officials everywhere, seated behind mahogany desks in marble-columned buildings, were prone to firing off memos that dictated laws and customs as biased as those propounded by Klansmen and race-baiting politicians enforcing Jim Crow laws.

I never had the chance to talk about any of this with my father. He didn't bring it up, so I had no occasion to press him. Until I pored over his military file, my appreciation of his time in uniform was faint. I wonder how he described his service in his letters to his mother, father, or five brothers. I've combed through letters written by other black servicemen to get a sense of how, in a segregated military, they saw their country and themselves in the fight for human rights overseas.

For the most part, these men were at once patriotic and frustrated. An anonymous letter to the editor of the *Pittsburgh Courier,* sent by a private in the 47th Quartermaster Regiment, Company D, illustrates the point: "If ever there were a time that all racial prejudices and hatred should be put aside, now it is at hand, and the country should be unified in every possible respect. . . . Negroes like the whites are quitting their jobs to increase the military strength of this Nation, because we all think that a nation worth being in is worth fighting for. But in the view of this so called Unity and National emergency the age old Monster of Prejudice has raised its head high."[8]

In March 1944, the *New Republic* printed another soldier's letter, one of several it had received about bias in the military.

The editors chose it because they believed it expressed a common sentiment: "Those of us who are in the armed services are offering our lives and fortunes, not for the America we know today, but for the America we hope will be created after the war."[9]

9
The Shooting

LIKE HIS FELLOW COUNTRYMEN, my father participated in the war effort to help win the four fundamental freedoms spelled out by President Franklin D. Roosevelt: freedom of speech, freedom of religion, freedom from want, and freedom from fear. But there was no freedom from want in Birmingham after the war, when Belvin Norris Jr. returned during the winter of 1946.

Although Birmingham's economy had flourished because of increased wartime industrial production, life on the home front still demanded sacrifice. The city, like much of the country, was triumphant in spirit, even as virtually every material resource was stretched to the limit. Sugar, steel, butter, lumber, cotton, and corn were all in short supply.

Even clothing was a hot commodity, especially menswear. Tens of thousands of returning veterans needed to swap their uniforms for civilian clothes, but stores couldn't get their hands on enough merchandise. At the outset of 1946, the government called on retail merchants to reserve hard-to-find garments for returning servicemen, whenever possible. Suits, overcoats, shirts, and underwear were to be set aside in "substantial proportions" for exclusive sale to veterans, noted the Civilian Production Administration, which also asked veterans, in turn, to limit their buying to their "immediate needs."

If returning white soldiers were having a hard time finding civilian clothes, the difficulty was compounded for black veterans. Even in those retail establishments where they were allowed to shop, they were denied the use of dressing rooms, as prescribed by segregation laws. Civilian clothes were in such short supply that some returning black veterans had to avail themselves of coveralls, jumpsuits, castoffs from mine workers, or hand-me-downs from church congregants—garments that were an insult to their pride and a reminder of their second-class citizenship.

There were shortages of everything. Meat was so scarce that fistfights broke out in butcher shops. The desperation in Birmingham was akin to what was going on all over the country. One widely printed newspaper story told of a melee outside a Philadelphia shop. A mob formed when word spread that the butcher had acquired generous cuts of prime meat. After much screaming and chanting by the mob outside, the rattled proprietor finally opened the door and tried to explain that he had only a single leg of lamb. A buxom woman shoved him aside and pushed her way in, grabbed the leg of lamb, and used it to bludgeon her way to the cash register.

In 1946, President Harry Truman asked for even more belt-tightening in the United States to avoid what he called "mass starvation" overseas. Under Truman's directive, wheat could no longer be used as livestock feed or to make hard alcohol or beer. And a greater portion of the wheat kernel was retained, producing flour darker and grainier than what was customary in the spongy, store-bought bread Americans loved. The government was so worried that people would rebel against this change in their eating habits that the president, with the help of Department of Agriculture home economists, staged a taste test for the White House press corps, hoping to sell the country on the idea that dark bread was more healthful than white.

Clothing and food shortages were the least of it for black veterans, who returned to civilian life more acutely aware of the disparity between America's promise of freedom and its continued practice of racial segregation. In the mid-1940s, Birmingham, Alabama, was a place where even the best-dressed black man might have to step off the sidewalk if a white person—regardless of class—was heading in his direction. Strict segregation ruled all aspects of city life. Bathrooms, water fountains, restaurants, waiting rooms, public transportation, and private hospitals were all divided along the color line; only the boldest or most desperate dared to cross it. When asked to describe the racial climate in Birmingham, a local branch officer for the NAACP said that blacks in his city were "gripped with an almost paralyzing fear."[1]

Birmingham was a city of boundaries, warnings, exhortations. Ministers preaching of brotherly love also insisted on the necessity to keep the Negro in his place. If the minister was a Negro, he might advise his congregants against trusting even the most benevolent white person. Black children were advised to lower their eyes and their voices when speaking to white adults, and white children learned that certain simple courtesies were never to be offered to a Negro. Nor was a Negro to be called "Mr." or "Mrs.," much less "sir" or "ma'am." If respect was due because of age or affection or trust, then a Negro worker should be addressed as "Auntie," "Uncle," "Nanny," "Mammy," or by a first name. The white child was instructed that the world of white privilege would tilt off its axis if he or she called a dutiful family employee Mr. Otis or Mrs. Ella Mae or used any other form of address proper only for whites.

The code for blacks was strict and unforgiving, held in place by the unspoken though ever-present threat of loss of income, dignity, or even life. In her memoir *The Wall Between,* the activist and former journalist Anne Braden tells of a memorable conversation she had with a man from an older generation. She describes him as one of the kindest men she had ever known, someone she had always admired for his gentle spirit and courtly ways and the respect he showed to people of color. Nonetheless, she says, he embraced segregation with "a violence that squared with nothing else in his personality." When she suggested to him that an anti-lynching law might be a good idea, his response was abrupt and caustic, intended to stifle such foolishness on the part of a "well-bred" southern girl. He told her, "We have to have a good lynching every once in a while to keep the nigger in his place."[2]

Much later Braden would reveal that the courtly gentleman was her father. And while she was convinced that he would never have joined a lynch mob, she nonetheless concluded that he had already "committed murder in his heart and mind" by voicing a sentiment that had "sprung out of the unconscious places of his soul."

In film and literature and elsewhere in popular culture, segregationists are often portrayed as grotesque caricatures warped by hate and aggression. But in reality the Jim Crow system was held firmly in place by fear on both sides of the color line; fear of diminished social status, lessened earning potential, or cheap, exploitable labor was as keenly felt as fear of white retaliation or loss of dignity. Both whites and blacks had to live according to a strict racial hierarchy.

Consider the tight vise of Birmingham's racial system when my father returned from the war. Imagine downtown, not as it is now, with its smattering of hotels and sandwich shops, but as it was in the mid-1940s. Because of wartime production, Alabama's urban population had grown by 57 percent, as tens of thousands left rural towns for industrial centers like Mobile, Montgomery, and Anniston.[3] As the state's largest city, Birmingham saw the biggest influx. After the Depression, Birmingham had turned into a boomtown, the downtown area reflecting the city's changing fortunes. It had a domed train station, neoclassical skyscrapers, and swank department stores like Porter's and Pizitz. The business district was abuzz day and night, with its early morning farmers' markets, midday retail rush, and crowded nightclubs and church revivals in the evening.

Though downtown brought blacks and whites together and they walked the same streets, everyone observed racial demarcations. Blacks knew which restaurants offered service through a side window and which buildings had colored restrooms or drinking fountains. Only certain stores allowed colored customers to try on hats, gloves, or clothing before buying them, though the courtesy was never advertised. Birmingham's strict segregation had facilitated the emergence of a thriving black business corridor, just beyond downtown's main retail center. Originally settled by Jewish families, Fourth Avenue evolved into the lifeline of the black merchant class. It was the main artery of a network of juke joints, dance halls, beauty shops, real estate agencies, and restaurants. You could pose for a picture at Brown's studio, as my father and his brothers often did, or you could stop by to see Bishop B. G. Shaw, an entrepreneurial clergyman who could fix you up from head to toe—he owned Shaw's Beauty Salon and Shaw's Shoe Store. At the Little Savoy Cafe, ten cents would get you a strong cup of coffee, and for twenty-five cents you could have a fried chicken dinner with a choice of three sides. The food in the Fourth Avenue district was legendary and its gravitational pull so strong that prestigious white families who would never set foot in a Negro restaurant quietly dispatched emissaries with wooden boxes or straw baskets to sneak in and out for large orders to go.

Lawyers, doctors, dentists, and other professionals were clustered in one of two tall buildings, the black community's pillars of self-respect: the seven-story Beaux Arts limestone Masonic Temple at 1630 Fourth Avenue and the six-story brick Pythian Temple. Their names suggest ornateness, but, save for the arched windows or Corinthian columns, the two looked like most office buildings constructed around the turn of the twentieth century. While modest by today's standards, they were considered skyscrapers at the time. Both had been designed by a black architect and built by a black-owned construction company. For a time, the Pythian Temple housed one of the first black-owned financial institutions in the United States, the Alabama Penny Savings Bank, later sold to the Grand Lodge of the Knights of Pythias, a service organization.

Both buildings had spaces for social gatherings, entertainment, and civic organizing. The Masonic Temple housed the first lending library open to blacks; the NAACP had offices on its sixth floor; and the Southern Negro Youth Congress was headquartered on the fourth. In addition to its professional offices, the Pythian Temple boasted a private waiters' club, where its meticulously groomed manager, Johnnie Perkins, looked down his nose over his pencil-thin mustache and decided who got in and who didn't.

The Pythian Temple is at the corner of Eighteenth Street and Third Avenue, across from the rear entrance of the Alabama Theatre and a few blocks from the Tutwiler hotel and the Sixteenth Street Baptist Church. As a child, I frequently passed the building on the way to the train station or a downtown department store, whizzing by, my forehead pressed against the car window. And though, from the front seat, my relatives would offer running commentary about city landmarks and who did what on this or that corner, no one ever once referred to the melee involving my father at the Pythian Temple on the night of February 7, 1946. Had I been older or more perceptive, I might have caught some discomfiture in my relatives' speech or demeanor, as we rushed along the building's sidewalk on our way to fetch new church gloves to replace the ones I was forever misplacing or soiling beyond repair. The Pythian Temple had no special place in the narrative of our lives, even though it was where my father, Belvin, and his brother Woody had been arrested.

When I first started asking questions about the shooting and arrest, I discovered that my mother had learned about the incident—much as I did and at around the same time—to her great surprise, from a cousin who had blabbed about it at a family funeral. While the revelation had made me want to scream with frustration, my mother initially dismissed the story as "crazy talk." She shrugged her shoulders, no doubt adding the tale to her catalog of possible explanations for the failure of her marriage to Belvin. She didn't know anything about it, and saw no reason to bother herself with knowing more. "You believe what you need to believe about your parents," she told me. "It's what we all do, and that belief has served you well in your life, so please don't go looking for old ghosts."

I wondered if Mom, too, had had her own epiphanies and how she had coped with the fact that Dad had walled off a part of his life. How could she not have known? How could she have traveled to Alabama repeatedly and never heard anything about this from her husband or his parents? Grandpa Belvin treated Mom like a queen. He called her "Daughter" as if that were her first name, and for a man who had six sons, it was a term of endearment. Yet in all those long talks on the front porch in Birmingham, it never came up? How could it be that, in their intimacy, the husband and wife on Oakland Avenue had never spoken of this? And had she known, would it have made a difference? I suppose I should have known better than to expect a simple yes or no to that question from Mom. Instead she said, "It would have explained a lot."

Untangling what had happened at the Pythian proved extremely difficult. My grandparents and four of my father's five brothers had passed away. Only Joe, the youngest, remained to give sketchy recollections of what he'd heard. He had been away in the military when the shooting happened. He wasn't at the house when Dad and Woody ventured out for the evening and returned home from jail twenty-four hours or so later.

When my father and his brother left Ensley for downtown Birmingham that fateful evening, they were with their fellow classmate John Beaton, as the police docket suggested. Beaton's parents, Abe and Jesse, lived two doors down from my grandparents; the two women, Jesse and Fannie, were particularly close. If I could track John Beaton down, I thought, he might be able to tell me exactly what had happened in the Pythian elevator. But I soon discovered that John Beaton had died years ago. My next idea was to find one of his siblings, who might have lived on Avenue G back in February of '46, in the hope that they remembered the hubbub the shooting most certainly would have caused.

John Beaton had two brothers: Morris, known as Mott, and Abe, named for his father. Like my father and uncles, the Beaton men had moved north—in their case, to Chicago—in search of better opportunities. I reached Abe on a Thursday morning and immediately regretted placing the call so early. It's hard to get information from anyone jolted from sleep by a ringing phone. And since Abe Beaton was eighty-five years old, I imagined a heavy, old-fashioned rotary phone whose ring could be heard throughout his building. Groggy as he was, he softened when I mentioned the name Norris, but his familiarity with the incident didn't yield much. His speech was slow and somewhat slurred; in response to my appeals he couldn't offer any firsthand information. He seemed to believe it was still 1946 and he was in the army. The more we talked, the more he appeared eager to get back to bed. I thanked him and said good-bye.

I tried to reach his brother Morris repeatedly, with no success. Just when I was ready to give up, Uncle Joe remembered another Beaton relative—Julia, much younger than her brothers. When I got her on the phone, I had no idea what I was in for.

Julia Beaton had been five years old in 1946, and while she could not remember the specifics of the incident involving my dad, she recalled a chaotic evening that winter that had left her parents wary of police cars cruising through the neighborhood.

She suggested that I try her brother Morris and gave me his cell phone number, noting that it was a much better way to reach him than his house phone. I was grateful for the tip, but before I let her go, I asked, "What do you remember about life in Birmingham?"

There was a long pause, then sniffles. She said she needed a moment; I heard her set the phone down. Soon she returned to the line and asked me if I had time to hear her out. "Let me tell you one of my strongest memories," she said. "I remember your grandparents walking home, all in white. They were coming home from church. Probably a revival, because they had white on head to toe. And I remember some kids. Some white kids came zoomin' down the street hanging out of car windows and they pelted them with rotten tomatoes. They threw tomatoes at churchgoing folks and they laughed and they called them names I am not going to say out loud. Their clothes were ruined and they were so upset. Those kids in that car were just evil. What happens to make young people feel that kind of evil so early in life? I have never forgotten that. People do what they can get away with, and in Birmingham they could get away with anything. My feelings toward Birmingham, toward white people, are wrapped up in what happened that day when those boys threw those tomatoes at folks coming home from Sunday prayer."

I was startled by her raw candor. It was the first time I'd ever spoken to Julia Beaton, and my question about life in the South had burst open a dam. "I don't talk about this, and I barely know why I am talking about this now," she said. "I am not a prejudiced person, but I do not trust American white people. When you have seen people treated that way and hurt and the shooting and the bombings and the constant disrespect, it bothers me. It really bothers me to this day. The theaters had an upstairs part for black folks, and you needed to go up front and pay and then go outside again and up the back stairs to get to your seats. All so they could just remind you what they really thought of you. On the buses they sometimes had boards to keep people from sitting certain places even if seats were available. I am sixty-eight, and I remember it just like it was yesterday. I can't look at these civil rights documentaries, because it is not entertainment and it sure as hell ain't ancient history."

I had planned on this being a quick phone call, but Julia didn't give me a chance to interject. She was gathering steam, a freight train of rage: "I have no white American friends. I just don't care for them. I just don't trust them. I have always told my sons and my grandsons not to bring a woman in this house who does not look like me. That is a point of respect. I have a problem with the entertainers and the athletes. Sidney Poitier and Quincy Jones. They can do what they want, but it was a sign of disrespect to black women everywhere."

I heard Julia Beaton exhale loudly, and I could almost imagine her slumping in exhaustion on the other end of the line. "Listen," she said, commanding my attention. "I am not a mean person, but I am very firm in what I believe in. Birmingham was a very scarring place. Nothing per se happened to me. It was just the things you heard about that happened to other people. Everything for you was less than it was for other people, and though it is better today, my grandsons hate . . . and I say *hate* white people."

Julia went on to explain that her grandsons' anger had resulted from their encounters with the police. They are car enthusiasts, she said, and they like to spend hours tricking out their automobiles with spoilers and flashy chrome grilles. This leads police in their hometown to mistakenly assume they're members of a street gang. It never occurs to the police, she said, that they're young men who work full-time, go to church every Sunday, and spend their free hours tinkering with cars in the garage.

I asked her if she was bothered that her grandsons are consumed by hatred for whites. I suggested to her that hatred is hardly admirable, especially on the part of worshipful churchgoers. She agreed, though only to a point, saying, "I know that hatred can do more harm to you than to the other person, but frankly, I understand what they feel."

After twenty-five minutes on the phone with Julia, I was reeling. I felt honored by her frankness. But despite our shared history on Avenue G, she was far more distraught and full of rage about Birmingham than anyone in my immediate family has ever been—anyone related by blood to the churchgoing couple pelted with rotten tomatoes by young white hoodlums or to the serviceman shot by a Birmingham policeman.

This anger and mistrust, the absolute disdain for members of another race, the hatred: these were the very sentiments that civil rights marchers in 1963 had tried to overcome. But if there is one thing I have learned while listening closely to hidden conversations about race in America, it is how complex that objective really was. Many people of color wanted to move the country forward, wanted to convince white people, by moral suasion, no longer to hate and subjugate black America, while they themselves secretly clung to festering, old grudges, the better to foster communal solidarity.

You rarely hear the kind of loathing freely expressed by Julia Beaton. But sentiments like hers, if aired, would likely elicit empathy or understanding among black and even some white Americans, for they are rooted in abysmal pain caused by racial strife. A white American voicing such raw feelings would likely be met with swift condemnation and a demand for an apology. But hate is hate. Disgust is almost always a damaging emotion, and contempt eats away at the soul, no matter who you are.

Race is often seen as a black issue in America. When any institution puts together a panel or symposium or committee on race or diversity, you can be sure that it will focus on reaching out to, hearing from, or being more inclusive of people of color. Reluctance among whites to talk about race and discomfort when doing so are usually seen as the chief obstacles to progress. Less explored is the legacy of distrust black parents pass on to their children. Many of us are advised by our elders to beware of whites. Rare is the black boy who has not been told to be on guard in all encounters with white police officers. This advice comes in many forms. Sometimes it's subtle. Sometimes severe. Sometimes it's imparted through humor.

"You have to be twice as good to go half as far"; "Never give a white person a reason to question your honesty"; or, as Michael Smith of York, Pennsylvania, told me, a large black man has to be mighty jolly in the workplace. This kind of advice can be corrective but also corrosive. It's as if one is being counseled to reject membership in a club before it rejects you. Some call this "keeping it real" but it can also lead to complicity in your own oppression. Here a certain honesty can slide into the muck of race. Can a black woman who tells her son to be wary of blond teachers or white police officers be sympathetic to a blond mother who warns her daughter to lock the car doors when she drives through black neighborhoods?

As I listened to Julia Beaton, the mystery of my father's story deepened. He'd done more than keep it to himself. He'd kept his anger, frustration, or shame—or whatever he'd felt that night in the elevator of the Pythian Temple—locked away in a secret place. Julia had displayed more anger on behalf of the Norrises than I had ever witnessed from him. How, I wondered, had my father been able to find balm for the emotional wound from his encounter with the Birmingham police?

By the time I'd reached junior high school, our neighborhood was dotted with black men who were committed to family life. They coached sports and donned aprons for backyard barbecues. On Saturdays, they washed their cars by hand so that the chrome would sparkle like a pinkie ring when they drove their families to church the next day. But if you watched these

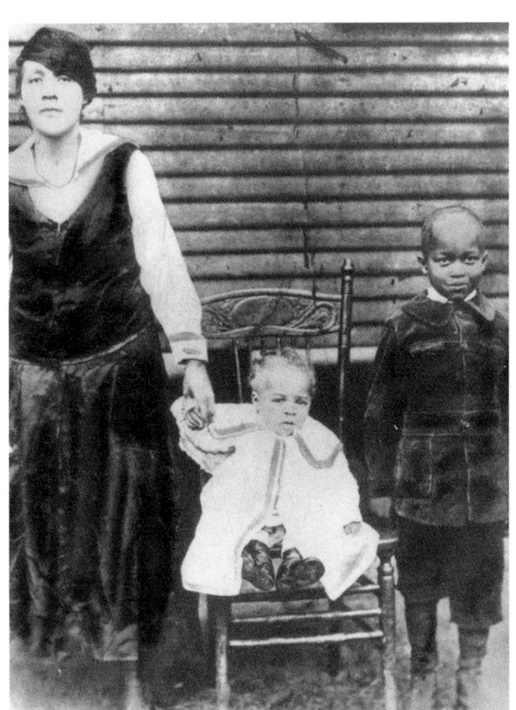

Grandma Fannie Norris
with her two eldest sons,
Louis (seated) and
Sylvester Wallace

Grandma Fannie and Grandpa Belvin Sr.:
their church directory photo

The six Norris brothers (clockwise from upper left):
Belvin (wearing the darkest suit jacket), Joe Nathan, Louis,
Woodrow, Simpson, and Sylvester Wallace

Grandma Ione and Grandpa Jinx Brown in front of their home
in Minneapolis before heading to my cousin Roy's wedding ceremony

Only Negro Alexandria High Graduate Portrays Version of 'Aunt Jemima'

Hundreds of Pancakes Served Here Friday By Former Ione Hopson

The only Negro girl to graduate from Alexandria high school returned to her old home town last Friday as the celebrated Minnesota version of "Aunt Jemima."

Ione Brown, formerly Ione Hopson, whipped up hundreds of her famous pancakes for shoppers at the Mel Johnson grocery Friday and in the course of doing so met a number of old classmates and other acquaintances here.

A charming, genial woman of ample proportions, (Ione says she got the job as Aunt Jemima because of her size and not her voice), she is both proud and happy with her new role in life.

Ione has been the Upper Midwest Aunt Jemima for the past three years. She was "discovered" by the Quaker Oats company while singing at the Bethesda Baptist church in south Minneapolis.

"The original Aunt Jemima is in Chicago," Ione explained. "I just sort of pinch hit for her in Minnesota, North and South Dakota, Michigan, Iowa and Wisconsin."

MRS. IONE BROWN

Grandma Ione Brown featured in a northern Minnesota newspaper, the *Park Region Echo*, on October 5, 1950. She was forty-seven years old.

My grandmother Ione Brown and my mother standing in their neighbor's yard. My mother is about nine years old and is frowning for reasons she can't remember.

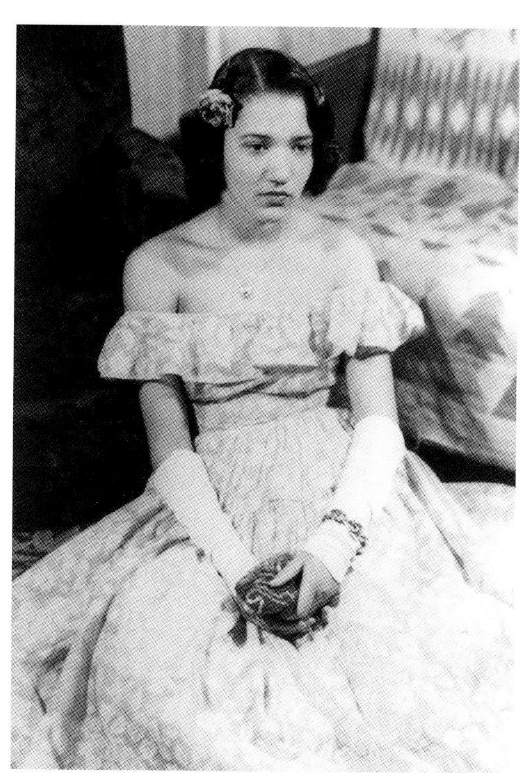

Mom before a high-school dance, wearing a hand-made gown

Mom standing on the steps of the Capitol in Washington, D.C., in April 1972, during one of our vacations

My favorite picture of my father

Belvin and Betty Norris dressed to the nines
in their new home on Oakland Avenue
in South Minneapolis

My sister Marguerite McGraw,
in her high-school graduation portrait

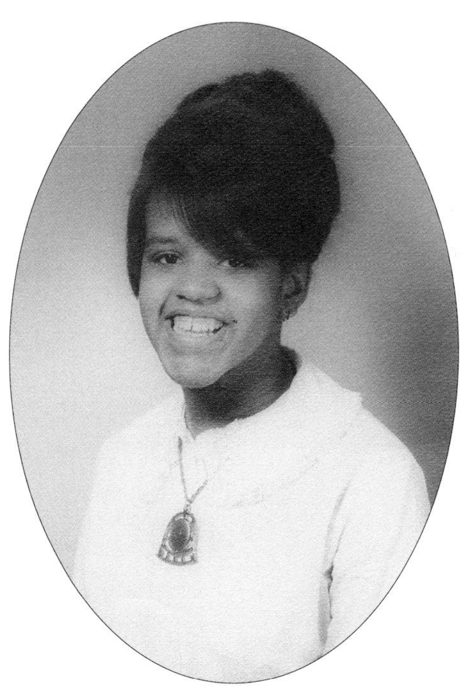

My sister Cindy McGraw,
in her eighth-grade school photo

Mom and me in Pensacola, Florida, in March 1972. This is Mom's Jackie O. photo; she's slim, chic, the wind blowing her hair.

Father and daughter in our "family portrait"

My eighth-grade school photo.
This was my mother's idea
of a "sporty" hairdo.

A teenaged Belvin Norris at Camp Robert Smalls,
the Naval Station at Great Lakes, Illinois

NEGRO NEGRO 9b

Name NORRIS, Belvin, Jr.
(Name in Full, Surname to the Left)

605 85 79 (Service No.) AS (Rate) USN ☐ USNR ☒ V-6 (Class)

Date Reported Aboard: 9 August, 1943

NRS. Birmingham, Alabama
(Present Ship or Station)

First Enlistment ☒ Reenlistment ☐

(Ship or Station Received From)

Enlisted ☒ Reenlisted ☐ 9 August, 1943 (Date)

To Serve 2 (Years)

Construction Battalion ☐

Placed on Active ☒ Inactive ☐ Duty This Date

D.S.S. Form 166 Submitted ☒

Authority:

Remarks:

FOR USE OF RECRUITING STATIONS ONLY

6

Recalled to Active Duty (Date)

Transferred 9 August, 1943 (Date)

To US NAVTRASTA Great Lakes, Illinois

C. S. CARROLL, LIEUT, USNR
Signature and Rank of Commanding Officer

Date Received Aboard: 10 AUG 1943

USNTS GREAT LAKES, ILL.
(New Ship or Station)

USNRS BIRMINGHAM, ALA.
(Last Ship or Station)

R.R.M. EMMET, Captain, USN
Signature and Rank of Commanding Officer.

ORIGINAL
FOR SERVICE RECORD

U.S. Navy Enlistment Form noting that Belvin Norris would serve under class V-6 (Negro)

Eugene "Bull" Connor, his wife, Beara, and their daughter, Jean
(*Birmingham, Alabama, Public Library Archives, Portrait Collection*)

Belvin and Woodrow Norris posing for a professional photographer at a social event early in the winter of 1946, most likely days or even hours before the shooting at the Pythian Temple

A few months before she died, Aunt Blanche mailed me this undated photo of Belvin and Woody

After parading through the streets of Birmingham, World War II veterans pose for a photo in front of the Jefferson County Courthouse, before entering to assert their right to vote. The campaign was organized by the Southern Negro Youth Congress Veteran's Committee. Chairman Henry O. Mayfield holds the sign that says, JOIN US TO REGISTER—BRING YOUR DISCHARGE PAPERS!

Dad and Woody in Chicago

Joe Norris

Dad and Mom attending one of my high-school games in 1979, probably toughing it out as a "couple" even though they lived apart

Mom and me in 1988, the year my father died

One of the enduring sorrows of my life is that my father never met my husband or my children, pictured here on the day my stepson graduated from college (from left): my son, Norris; my husband, Broderick Johnson; my stepson, Broddy; my daughter, Aja; and me.

men closely, you could see a certain brooding indignation that registered somewhere in a smile that seemed forced. It stemmed from the pain that comes with being admitted to a party only after you've forced your way in. That nagging disappointment arising from the knowledge that you weren't on the original guest list. Dad was the exception. If he'd harnessed anger, and I suspect that he had, its traces were not evident. I needed to understand the nature of his self-control in a life stunted by the savage forces of Jim Crow, yet ultimately blessed by good fortune as a result of his packing up and moving north.

I took Julia's advice and called Morris Beaton. He'd been born in 1928, two years after his brother John, who was with my father that night. When I finally reached Morris on his cell, there was no hesitation in his recall of the incident. He'd been home on Avenue G when his brother and the Norris brothers returned from jail, he told me. He remembered listening to them tell their story in breathless spurts, moving from the living room to the kitchen to the porch. John Beaton had grown up playing marbles and baseball with Woody and Belvin. Belvin and John had just returned from military service.

It was my father's second week back home. He had returned to Birmingham in late January, when the city and the entire state were riding high in the wake of the University of Alabama's decisive defeat of USC at the Rose Bowl. Wet, unseasonably cold weather had swamped the city since his homecoming, turning the red Alabama clay into a thick, forbidding soup. Woe to anyone who tracked it into my grandmother's house. She was a small, birdlike woman, always sporting a floral apron and clutching a household instrument in her small, delicate hands. A broom. A mop. A spatula. A hot comb for straightening hair. A switch to show the kids she meant business. She was feisty and forever fussing at her sons, as if her loving admonitions would follow them out the door as safeguards in a heartless world. I can see Woody and Belvin leaning down to kiss her good-bye, muttering dismissive "Yes, Mama's" as she chattered at them. I can hear her cackling southern purr, warning Belvin and Woody to avoid flashy women and stay out of trouble, as they ambled down the porch stairs for a night on the town.

During the second week of February, the bad weather ceased, and, as Morris Beaton tells it, Belvin, Woody, and Morris's brother John headed downtown to an event at a public park near the Smith and Gaston Funeral Home, before deciding to go to the Pythian Temple. "They used to have dances or parties or something up there. It was a get-together that they was having upstairs, and they were standing in the lobby there trying to wait for the elevator to come down before the police walked up," Morris explained.

"And when the police come up, they were behind them, but when the elevator door opened, a policeman stuck his stick out there where he wouldn't let them get on the elevator, and this is where your father knocked the stick down and stepped on the elevator, and this is where everything got started, the beating and the cursing and all that stuff. They got a good whupping that night."

The three young men were unarmed. The policemen, of course, were packing. Morris Beaton said he was told that one police officer reached for his gun after my father stood up to the cop who had tried to block their entrance to the elevator. My father physically tried to stop him from reaching for his holster. "When they was tussling on the elevator, this is when the gun went off," Beaton said. "The police was trying to get it, and Belvin was trying to keep, trying to keep him from getting it. 'Cause he had it in a holster."

Beaton said that John, Woody, and Belvin all described the shooting as accidental. When the police officer succeeded in pulling his gun out, it was pointed at my father's chest. Woody instinctively tried to knock the gun out of the cop's hand. Amid all the commotion, the gun discharged, the bullet grazing my father's leg.

The mishap aside, Morris wonders whether my father might have been killed had he not tried to prevent the policeman from reaching for his weapon. This seems far-fetched to me. More likely than not, the police intended only to put some black men in their place, not six feet under.

In retrospect, it is conceivable that the five white police officers in the Pythian Temple lobby might have been almost as spooked by the unfolding incident as the black men they tried to stop from getting on the elevator. They were outnumbered—the building was full of blacks—and in the heart of the black business district. The sound of a gun going off could have made for an explosive situation that Thursday night; the police officers had no idea how many people had gathered for the event upstairs.

When word of the incident first reached Avenue G, my grandfather and John Beaton's father assessed the risks of heading to the jail where their sons were incarcerated. They feared that the police might embroil them in the affair and throw them in jail as well. Instead, Grandma Fannie called a lawyer she knew from her work at the hospital to help get Woody, Belvin, and John released. Sylvester and Simpson Norris, meanwhile, started putting money together to make bond for their brothers. There was urgency, Morris Beaton said, to get the two men out of jail as fast as possible. "Some awful, terrible things happened to black men when they were behind bars with them police. They had total control and no one to answer to. They wouldn't want them to be in that jail for one second longer than they had to be there."

The gunshot wound, Morris stressed, was superficial and did not require hospitalization. And though he didn't say it outright, the way he told the story suggested that when Woody and Belvin got home, they faced some rough justice from their father, because Belvin senior was certain that he'd raised his sons to know better than to smack at a policeman's hand—even if they felt the need to demand respect as men. "They didn't talk much about it after that," Morris said. They stayed away from downtown and eventually left town. "They wanted to move out and get out on their own," he added. "Go to some better state, better place, I mean where people would be treated equal and everything else."

I asked Morris a question I wished I had been able to ask my father: "As a black man, what mind-set could have provoked you to go up against a Birmingham police officer like that back then?" "Well, you would have had to be in the mind-set of getting shot or getting killed, going up against them," he replied. "I mean, they was extra mean to black people for some reason. I don't know why. They just act like they was better than everybody and they felt like they could do anything they wanted to do."

While unraveling my father's story, I interviewed other black veterans. I've come to understand how a man can break from character when he concludes that his dignity and self-worth are more important to him than anything else in life, regardless of the warnings, spoken or not, telling him where he can sit, sleep, shop, pee, work, ride, walk, learn, eat, pray, love, and live. These veterans had spent months proudly wearing the uniform of the most powerful military on earth. They were part of the campaign to protect human rights for all. They had learned to honor the uniform and themselves, and were keenly sensitive to freedom and fairness. There is a certain sparkle in a man's eyes when he describes that moment when he decided to let his spirit fly, to refuse to allow his dreams to be held in check, subjected to the whims of others. I've seen that sparkle in the eyes of black veterans who talked to me. I wish I'd seen it in my father's.

"Why do you think he never told me, his daughter, about

that evening?" I asked Morris. "Or never talked to my mother, his wife, about it?" "I have no idea, honey," he said. "I guess some things like that, I mean . . . people misuse you, abuse you. . . . I mean, it's better forgotten than to keep talking about it."

I don't think my father ever forgot that night. How can you forget the rush of adrenaline, the crack of a gunshot, the pain of your wound? Your harrowing ride in a police car, your thankful walk to freedom after a night in a Birmingham jail. The disapproving stare from your father as you try to explain why you swatted at a police officer's billy club. Surely Dad must have winced every time he spotted a police cruiser anywhere after that. Surely he must have remembered the trip to the courthouse to pay the fines three months later. Surely the lilt in his step, as a result of the gunshot, must have been a constant reminder of the incident. Why didn't you tell your children any of this when you took them "down South" to visit relatives?

I suppose that, like many veterans, Dad spent so much time trying to get beyond the unpleasantness of his military service that he also locked these memories away in his mind, much like the way he hid his medal and his navy photos. Maybe he feared that the telling of his ordeal on February 7, 1946, would so embitter his children as to compel them to hate whites, like Julia Beaton and her grandsons did. Dad taught us to look for goodness in everyone. Sharing that story might complicate or even undermine that lesson. Dad didn't seem to have ever been under the spell of that evening. He had suffered a superficial wound, and his dignity may have been singed. But he had managed to move on, willfully ignoring memories that were like a pebble in a shoe: painful at first, but at some point you just stop noticing it.

I suspect that Dad didn't feel special about having avoided a terrible fate when the policeman's gun discharged. He wasn't the only lucky one that evening. Had he been seriously harmed or even killed, the five white policemen would have had some explaining to do to their superiors, however accidental the happening; or they might even have been haunted into their sunset years by having killed a man. Ever the optimist, my father believed in a certain kind of kismet. To be sure, now and then he probably cursed the cop who shot him. But more often than not, he would have thought he did the guy a favor by living. I'm sure of that.

10

The War at Home

EVEN AFTER LEARNING ABOUT the incident at the Pythian Temple, I still don't know exactly what role my father's status as a veteran may have played in his shooting. I'm not even certain he was wearing a uniform at the time. Morris Beaton thinks he was wearing "sailor whites," but he cautioned me that he's not entirely sure.

Here is what I do know. My father had a violent confrontation with the policemen at a moment when two social forces were coming to a head in Alabama's largest city. Black veterans were returning to the Jim Crow South after having undergone a profound transformation in the service of their country. They were hungry for change, willing to take risks, and keen to assert themselves as men.

At the same time, the power base in Birmingham—the elected officials, who ruled by the ballot, and the segregationists, who ruled by terror—were hell-bent on maintaining the status quo. The postwar years thrust Birmingham into uncertain political waters. On the very day of my father's confrontation with police, the city's two main papers, the *Birmingham Age-Herald* and the *Birmingham News,* carried stories about a sudden swell of new voters. Jefferson County was bracing for ten thousand new registrants, and veterans accounted for about 75 percent of that figure.

The editorial page of the *Birmingham News* applauded the veterans for doing their civic duty in its February 7 afternoon edition: "This was to be expected, but it is highly gratifying to see them responding to this responsibility of civilian citizenship. It means that these men have come back from the Army eager to take part in community life. While only a few veterans have as yet jumped into the battle for office, one may feel reasonably sure that, in this large new portion of voters, there are many potential office seekers."

What the *Birmingham News* and other mainstream newspapers failed to acknowledge was the large pool of black veterans who were also eager to embrace their civic duty to vote—in the newspaper's words, "this responsibility of civilian citizenship."

Throughout January and February that winter, black men who had just returned from duty were descending on city hall, trying to register. My father was released from the navy on January 21, and the very week he returned to Birmingham, black veterans were defiantly parading through the downtown business district. On January 23, a group of black men made their way to the County Board of Registrar's office.

The postwar months were a season of parades, and the black veterans' march took place eleven days after the most memorable of the postwar processions. On January 12, the 82nd Airborne Division had led thirteen thousand men through a blinding blizzard of swirling ticker tape in downtown New York to celebrate America's victory in World War II. An estimated four million people had lined New York's "Canyon of Heroes" for the largest parade since General John Pershing had led the 1st Division along the same route in 1919.

Also on January 12, a group of men in a smoke-filled chamber in Montgomery, Alabama, reluctantly announced that "qualified Negroes" would be allowed to vote in what had previously been an all-white primary.[1] The members of the Alabama Democratic Executive Committee had been given little choice in the matter. In 1944, in *Smith v. Allwright,* the U.S. Supreme Court had determined that all-white primaries were unconstitutional. Black voters—long locked out of the voting process—

saw a grand opportunity to exercise their right, especially black veterans who had fought for democracy overseas.

The Southern Negro Youth Congress (SNYC) held city-wide registration clinics for veterans. Officially, there were two main requirements: (1) the ability to read and write any portion of the United States Constitution; and (2) ownership of three hundred dollars' worth of taxable property. SNYC, needless to say, focused on the first at their clinics, conducting classes about the Constitution and the history of the United States government.

On that Wednesday morning, January 23, eleven days after the 82nd Airborne's victory parade down Fifth Avenue, black veterans in Birmingham held their own. Instead of thousands marching, there were dozens. But while the size of their gathering was minuscule in comparison, they nonetheless made a large and loud statement by stepping out of the roles prescribed for them by Alabama segregation. Henry O. Mayfield, the chairman of the Southern Negro Youth Congress, was among those who led the group, carrying a large white sign that read, JOIN US TO REGISTER—BRING YOUR DISCHARGE PAPERS![2]

There it was. Discharge papers. Just like the folded document my father had on his person the night of his confrontation with the police. The sign calling for discharge papers is clearly visible in a photograph of the black veterans. Before going into the courthouse, the men had stopped to pose for a picture. There are about sixty in the picture, almost all of them dressed in overcoats and fedoras. Most are smiling broadly. Some have their hands tucked into trousers with knife-edge pleats. A few are wearing work clothes and floppy hats of the kind that protect farmers from the sun. They, too, are smiling. All are radiant with possibility, staring at the camera as if tilting against the weight of history.

I yearn to know if my father was among those men who

marched to that plaza in front of the courthouse. The boldest among them assembled for a photo. Others hung back on the street, concerned that the photo might appear on the front page of newspapers and invite the ire of their bosses, their families, the city police, or even the Klan. Those who posed that day stood on the steps beneath these words of Thomas Jefferson's, inscribed in stone atop the courthouse door: EQUAL AND EXACT JUSTICE TO ALL MEN OF WHATEVER PERSUASION. Years later and thousands of miles away from Birmingham, my father used to carry a pocket-sized version of the U.S. Constitution in his back pocket, along with his wallet and an Afro pick. I am ashamed to say that I teased him about that when I was a teenager. It was one of his little eccentricities, and though I ribbed him about it, he always got the last word by hitting me with some specific constitutional question about section this from article that. And when I tried to laugh away the fact that I could not provide an answer, I'd get his standard retort: "Listen, girl: ignorance is no laughing matter."

That little brown book takes on a whole new meaning now, as does the collection of I VOTED stickers I found in his dresser drawer after he died. He got those oval stickers whenever he went to Eugene Field Elementary School in South Minneapolis to cast his ballot. A former neighbor once reminisced about how he and my father used to ride the bus to and from their jobs in downtown Minneapolis, both toting lunch in brown paper bags. Though Dad kept a series of simple yet beautifully maintained cars, he would not dream of driving downtown to pay for parking when he could spend a fraction of the money on bus fare. While people on the bus were reading paperbacks or the *Minneapolis Star and Tribune,* Mr. Johnson said, my father would sometimes reach inside his back pocket, pull out his little brown copy of the Constitution, and lose himself in its pages until the bus pulled up to Forty-ninth and Chicago.

I wonder if he was drawn to Amendment 15, Section 1: "The right of citizens of the United States to vote shall not be denied or abridged by the United States or by any State on account of race, color, or previous condition of servitude." Or perhaps the 24th Amendment: "The right of citizens of the United States to vote in any primary or other election for President or Vice President, for electors for President or Vice President, or for Senator or Representative in Congress, shall not be denied or abridged by the United States or any State by reason of failure to pay any poll tax or other tax."

I imagine a young Belvin Norris in the weeks after he arrived in Birmingham from serving his country. In my mind's eye I can see him busying himself with study of the laws of this great land, assiduously preparing to assert his right to vote. For this was a grand obsession in black Birmingham, the subject of sermons, talk at the dinner table, and chatter in barbershops, the background noise wherever blacks spoke freely about their ambitions. Whites in Birmingham might have sensed a shift in attitude had they been privy to the goings-on in black Birmingham's inner sanctums. They would have heard talk of a new day coming; they would have heard men and women reciting the Constitution or quizzing each other on the formation of government. In the restrooms or phone booths in the black business district along Fourth Avenue, they would have seen posters trumpeting a single word spelled out in heavy letters: VOTE!

Readers of the *Birmingham World,* which touted itself as "Alabama's largest Negro newspaper," were reminded of their civic responsibility with every new edition. A small box appeared in each issue, just under the masthead, alongside the subscription rates and a message from the managing editor, Emory O. Jackson. Inside that box readers would spy a message from President Franklin D. Roosevelt:

THE RIGHT TO VOTE.

"The right to vote must be open to all citizens irrespective of race, color or creed—without tax or artificial restriction of any kind. The sooner we get to that basis of political equality, the better it will be for the country as a whole."

The authoritative eloquence of the president ran smack into a white wall of resistance in the South, particularly in Birmingham, where considerable energy had been spent to ensure that the voting booth was closed to people of color.

In Alabama at that time, fewer than four thousand blacks had the right to vote, a tiny fraction of the state's black population. If blacks were suddenly allowed to rush to the ballot box, it would likely upset the state's power structure. State lawmakers moved quickly to slam that door by proposing the Boswell Amendment in 1945. The measure, named for State Senator E. C. "Bud" Boswell, was crafted "as a device for eliminating negro applicants." It gave local registrars broad powers to screen prospective voters with a test, under which citizens would have to prove that they understood and could explain any randomly selected section of the U.S. Constitution.

Using the slogan "Vote white, vote right," Alabama's Democratic Party stoked racial fears by warning that blacks would "take over if the amendment loses." Boswell Amendment supporters said it was "the only means short of intimidation" for white people in Alabama to preserve their political dominion. Dixiecrat demagogue Horace Wilkinson was unapologetic in explaining his unwavering support: "No Negro is good enough, and no Negro will ever be good enough to participate in making the laws under which the white people in Alabama have to live."[3]

On January 23, 1946, Birmingham's black veterans must have caused quite a scene as they assembled to register to vote. These black men proudly approached the courthouse, marching up the walkway and into the building in lockstep formation, four abreast. Inside, amid the bustle of other citizens paying their poll tax or registering, white and Negro registrants formed separate queues outside room 102.

According to news accounts, after waiting in line for hours, a substantial number of black veterans were turned away. Some were told that they had failed to fill out their paperwork properly. Others were denied because they could not "interpret" excerpts from the U.S. Constitution or provide correct answers to questions ranging from "What is meant by veto power in the U.N.?" to "How many suds are in a bar of soap?" Captain H. C. Terrell, an army chaplain who'd led the delegation, was taken into custody by military police for "using his Army uniform for political activities," but other than that, the voters' rights demonstration was peaceful and without incident.

The bold ambition of the black veterans inflamed local politicians and newspaper columnists, and the voting efforts were of grave concern to the Birmingham police—the force that Alabama power brokers relied on to keep black aspirations in check.

Decades before the glare of television cameras would make Birmingham police chief Eugene "Bull" Connor the bogeyman of the city's civil rights protests for turning dogs and hoses on youthful demonstrators, Connor had already built a national reputation as a fierce segregationist. In the 1940s he had been a particularly fierce opponent of the federal government's meddling with a state's right to determine and enforce its laws and customs. The police commissioner's passionate concern for states' rights and his prodigious ego are both on display in a letter he wrote to President Roosevelt, dated August 7, 1942. On city-issued stationery hailing Birmingham as the "Industrial Center of the South," Connor wrote:

My dear Mr. President

Re: RACIAL POLICIES

As Commissioner of Public Safety of the largest city in the State of Alabama, I feel that it is my patriotic duty to call to your attention a problem which is going to cause serious trouble unless abated by you, for there is no doubt that federal agencies have adopted policies to break down and destroy the segregation laws of this State and the entire South. Unless something is done quickly by you, we are going to face a crisis in the South, witness the annihilation of the Democratic Party in this section of the Nation, and see a revival of organizations which will usher in an era that will tend to destroy the progress made by law abiding white people, who have conscientiously labored to aid and help negroes to become better citizens.

The N.Y.A. has preached social equality and stirred up strife. The United States Employment Service and the Fair Employment Practices Committee are causing plenty of trouble when there ought to be unity. I can't see for the life of me why anyone should desire to start civil strife in the South when there is a war to be won, and the South is doing its part, as the record will disclose.

A large portion of our negroes have venereal disease, which, I think, is the number one problem of the negro race today, not Social Equality, as the agitators and some federal agencies are advocating. I believe in curing them, and we are making notable progress in this city. When the downfall of the doctrine of white supremacy is advocated and taught by agitators and federal officials, who know absolutely nothing about the negro problem in the South, what happens? Negroes become impudent, unruly, arrogant, law breaking, violent, and insolent. Any effort now by any person connected with the federal government officially or socially, to destroy segregation and bring about amalgamation of the races will hinder the Southland in its war efforts, revive organizations like the

> Ku Klux Klan, which I never joined, and result in lawlessness, disunity and probably bloodshed.
>
> You have made us a fine president. I am co operating [*sic*] with you one hundred percent. I have always voted for you, and I shall use all my energy, time and whatever influence I have to speedily carry out any plans you have for this district which will aid in winning the war. Don't you think one war in the South, however, is enough? Undoubtedly, this is no time for the federal government to meddle with racial problems, which every year, under the leadership of local authorities, improves and is being rapidly solved as satisfactorily as it [*sic*] can be settled.
>
> Mr. President won't you help us before it is too late.
>
> With kindest regards for you always, I am
>
> Respectfully yours,
> Eugene "Bull" Connor
> Commissioner of Public Safety[4]

The "racial problems" Connor spoke of most certainly applied to the rising tide of black veterans now eager to flex their muscles at the ballot box. Black men who had spent their lives being called "boys" returned to Birmingham from the war with a gust of pride that most certainly would have registered several degrees beyond uppity in Jim Crow's curious calculus of acceptable "negro behavior." Their status in the military had been stunted, but when they stepped off trains and buses upon their return home they were wearing the same uniforms as the white soldiers and sailors. (This fact underscored an equality of manhood, hinted at but not fully realized when black and white men donned business suits.) Those uniforms and a shared experience allowed the men a strut in their steps and a swell in their chests.

The black veterans posed a significant threat to the white power structure represented by Bull Connor—not only because of their numbers, but also because of their new willingness to challenge the Jim Crow system. The veterans and their service to country tugged at the heart of southerners worried that harsh segregation and Klan-led violence were tarnishing Alabama's reputation in the United States as well as abroad. White servicemen who'd traveled throughout Europe and the Pacific during the war had been dismayed to find that people an ocean away had come to view Alabama as a cauldron of racial hatred.

Meanwhile, the city's business community had its own set of worries. The defense contracts that had kept Birmingham's factories buzzing were one by one coming to an end. Attracting new business and new investors would prove difficult if groups like SNYC or the NAACP were successful in turning Birmingham into the principal battleground in the veterans' fight for voting rights.

To protect white power and preserve the southern way of life, Bull Connor's Birmingham Police Department reportedly tried to blunt the registration campaign by waging a private war against returning veterans. In the first two months of 1946, as many as half a dozen black veterans were reportedly killed by police officers from Birmingham and the surrounding communities.[5]

Though many have tried to unearth official evidence of police involvement in the killings, it has proved difficult, but the journalist–turned–civil rights activist Anne Braden has evoked the mood among police officers at the time in her memoir *The Wall Between*. In 1946, Braden was working as a newspaper reporter in Birmingham, covering the courthouse. There, she discovered "two kinds of justice, one for whites and one for Negroes." She explains, "If a Negro killed a white man, that was a capital crime. If a white man killed a Negro, there were usually extenuating circumstances."

Braden said she began to look the other way when she entered the courthouse on her way to work, so as not to see the phrase EQUAL AND EXACT JUSTICE carved in stone atop the building's door, which made a mockery of the proceedings inside. One particularly unsettling incident in the sheriff's office, she recalled, "almost tipped the scales of my sanity":

> The sheriff's office prided itself on its record of crime solution. I don't think it is as good as they said but they often boasted about it. One day, while I was killing time talking to some of the deputies, one of them said: "You know there's only been one murder in this county in the last two years that has never been solved."
>
> "And what was that?" I asked.
>
> "Come on, I'll show you," he said. He took me back into another room, opened a cabinet and took out a skull.
>
> "There it is," he said, setting the skull on the table. "And it never will be solved—that man was a nigger and he was killed by a white man."

Braden said she looked at the deputy and saw his eyes "twinkling not because he was joking but because he was talking of a conspiracy that pleased him, and of which he was a part, and which he evidently expected would please me too." She left without comment, terror-stricken.[6]

The civil rights activist Modjeska Simkins described an encounter with police chief Bull Connor that same year. After Connor and his force broke up a biannual meeting of the Southern Negro Youth Congress, Simkins and other SNYC leaders went to Connor's office on a Saturday to protest the way they had been treated. "As we went in, I guess that about thirteen white men were coming out," Simkins recalled. "This is 1946. And we went in there to see old Bull and he gave us no satisfaction. He said, 'You see those folks that just walked out of here? That's a leader from the Klan and they assured me that they would give me all the help I need.' "[7]

Perhaps this was why Jim Baggett had tried to lower my

expectations when I'd started looking into my father's brush with the Birmingham police. Though the killing of a half dozen black veterans in and around Birmingham by law enforcement had been widely reported over the years, the victims' names had rarely appeared in news stories or police reports. In fact, throughout the forties, blacks were rarely mentioned in white-owned newspapers, except when they committed crimes or there was extraordinary news to report about the black social or business elite. There was, however, a stark exception the week my father was shot.

Belvin and Woodrow Norris had their confrontation with the police on February 7, during the same six-week period when the six black veterans were allegedly murdered. After one night in jail they were released on Friday, February 8. And since their father, Belvin senior, always came home with a newspaper tucked under his arm, whether he was returning from work or from the shopping district, his two sons would have seen the headline in the *Birmingham News* when they picked up the evening paper on Saturday, February 9: EX-MARINE IS SLAIN, MOTORMAN INJURED IN STREETCAR ROW. The subhead explained, "Finding of justifiable homicide ruled in shooting of Negro by Police Chief."

A recently discharged black marine named Timothy Hood had reportedly moved the "segregation sign" separating the white and "colored" sections of a streetcar. When the motorman told him to stop, the ex-marine refused, and the two began to fight. As policemen arrived, the ex-marine fled and was later apprehended. While Timothy Hood sat in the back of the police car, he was shot in the head by the police chief of Brighton, a small city just outside Birmingham. Chief G. B. Fant would later explain that he lived near where the incident occurred and had responded because he'd heard a ruckus outside his home. Fant said he shot Hood because the ex-marine had made a sudden motion. Less than twenty-four hours later, Timothy Hood's death was ruled a justifiable killing.

The shooting of Timothy Hood only instances an epidemic of violence against black veterans in 1946 across the United States. Grisly news throughout the country dramatized the rough embrace of black soldiers after the war. That same February, a twenty-one-year-old navy veteran was flogged by a group of nine men near the Atlanta municipal airport.[8] Racial violence was not confined to the South, either. There was, for example, a triple shooting in Freeport, Long Island. Four Ferguson brothers were out on the town for a reunion. Richard Ferguson was an army veteran. Charles Ferguson, after returning from overseas duty, had just reenlisted. Joseph Ferguson was in the navy, serving as a ship's cook, third class. The fourth brother, Alonzo, was a civilian. When they were refused service at a coffee shop, they protested but left without incident. The coffee shop manager called the police to complain and warn about "misbehaving negroes"; shortly after that, the brothers were arrested by a white patrolman named Joseph Romeika.

According to eyewitnesses and court testimony, the four were lined up against a brick wall. When two of the brothers questioned their treatment, they were kicked in the groin. Two of the brothers, Charles and Alonzo Ferguson, were shot and killed by Romeika. Joseph Ferguson, the ship's cook, was shot in the shoulder. Though the rookie police officer claimed self-defense, his story was later dismissed by the U.S Navy, after it was determined that the victims had been unarmed when they were shot.

While New York governor Thomas Dewey was pressured to name a special prosecutor, black civil rights leader A. Philip Randolph kept bearing down on President Truman to show leadership by banning segregation in the armed forces. "I found Negroes not wanting to shoulder a gun for democracy abroad unless they get democracy at home," he told the *New York Times* on March 23, 1948. He asked the NAACP's legal committee to submit several amendments for incorporation into H.R. 4278, a pending bill advocating universal military training (UMT). Specifically, the amendments called for (1) prohibition of segregation and racial discrimination in all UMT programs; (2) a ban of discrimination and all racial segregation "in interstate travel for trainees in the UMT uniforms or any other military uniform"; (3) "making attacks on, or lynching of, a trainee in UMT uniform or a person in any other military uniform a federal offense"; (4) "banning the poll tax in federal elections for any trainee otherwise eligible to vote."[9]

An arm of the American Veterans Committee passed a resolution calling for a federal law to help protect black veterans: "Whereas, some 60 Negro soldiers were murdered in this country at the hands of irate fellow Americans . . . and, whereas the Department of Justice has not sought prosecution in a single case, moreover, the attorney general has declared himself helpless to proceed in such prosecutions: Be it resolved that the National Planning Committee of the American Veterans Committee recognizes the need of a federal law making an assault upon a man or a woman in uniform a federal offense." The resolution gained little support, and violence against black veterans continued for the rest of the year.[10]

In March, newspapers across the country carried stories about a race riot in Columbia, Tennessee, provoked by a fight between a black navy veteran and a white salesclerk. Ten people, including four white police officers, were wounded in the outbreak, and two black men were killed in a shooting inside the jail later that week.

In June, an army veteran named Etoy Fletcher was seized by four men, dragged into the woods, and beaten severely after he tried to register to vote in Brandon, Mississippi. After Fletcher filed a complaint with the police, Mississippi senator Theodore

Bilbo, in a broadcast campaign speech, called on every "red-blooded Anglo-Saxon man in Mississippi to resort to any means to keep hundreds of Negroes from the polls."[11]

In July, two black men, one of them a World War II veteran, were lined up near a secluded bridge in Monroe, Georgia, along with their wives, and shot dead by a large group of white men. The *New York Times* described the shooting as a massacre. The local coroner said that at least sixty bullets had been fired into the bodies of the two men and their wives. The women were sisters and had allegedly been killed because one had recognized a member of the mob.[12]

Among these incidents, one in particular stands out because its savage brutality sent shock waves across the country and eventually had an impact on President Truman's assessment of race issues in the military. The incident occurred less than a week after my father was shot. On the night of February 13, 1946, a black veteran, still wearing his uniform, was blinded by a South Carolina policeman hours after being discharged from the army. Isaac Woodard was twenty-seven years old and had just served fifteen months in the South Pacific. On February 12 he was discharged from Camp Gordon, in Georgia, and boarded a Greyhound bus to meet his wife and family in Winnsboro, South Carolina, where he was born. After the bus crossed over from Georgia into South Carolina, Woodard told bus driver A. C. Blackwell that he needed more time during a scheduled restroom stop. This request annoyed Blackwell, who claimed that he took particular offense at Woodard's saying he needed to "take a piss."

Later, Blackwell would explain that he told the veteran to sit down and be quiet, a command Woodard ignored. "God damn it," Woodard allegedly responded. "Talk to me like I'm talking to you. I'm a man just like you." The bus driver called ahead for police assistance, and two officers, Chief Lynwood Shull and Elliot Long, were waiting for Woodard when the Greyhound pulled into the sleepy hamlet of Batesburg, at the intersection of Granite and Railroad. When Woodard disembarked, they allegedly took him by the arm and led him to an alley around the corner from the bus stop.[13]

Woodard described what happened next in an affidavit:

> They didn't give me a chance to explain. The policeman struck me with a billy across my head and told me to shut up. After that the policeman grabbed me by my left arm and twisted it behind my back. I think he was trying to make me resist. I did not resist against him. He asked me, "Was I discharged?" And I told him, "Yes." When I said yes that is when he started beating me with a billy, hitting me across the top of the head. After that I grabbed his billy and wrung it out of his hand. Another policeman came up and drew his gun on me and told me to drop the billy or he'd drop me so I dropped the billy. After I dropped the billy, the second policeman held his gun on me while the other one was beating me. He knocked me unconscious. After I commenced to come to myself he yelled get up. I started to get up, he started punching me in my eyes with the end of the billy. When I finally got up he pushed me inside the jail house and locked me up. I woke up the next morning and could not see.[14]

The "billy" was of course a billy club—a nightstick loaded with lead pellets.

The testimony of others involved in the Batesburg incident differs from Woodard's. The bus driver said Woodard had been drinking and had offended his fellow passengers with his profanity, a charge Woodard and several others on the bus denied.[15] And though Woodard testified that he was struck in the eyes time and again by the nightstick, Chief Shull, who at first denied the charge, admitted to having administered a "single blow." "I'm sorry I hit him in the eye and blinded him," Shull told the jury at his trial that November. Shull said he'd had to act fast and did not have time "to pick a place to hit" Woodard. "I had no wish to blind anyone," Shull said. "I had no intention of hitting him in the eye, but I had to [hit] him in self defense because he was advancing on me." Shull also allowed that he might unwittingly have stuck a finger in Woodard's eye.

The full extent of Woodard's injuries was made public in December 1946 when a prisoner awaiting execution tried to bequeath his eyes to the blinded soldier. "I have a good pair of eyes which I want Isaac Woodard to have," wrote William H. Copeland from his jail cell.[16] At the behest of the NAACP, a team of prominent physicians examined Woodard for more than three hours to determine if a transplant was possible. Dr. Henry Gowens, who led the team, issued the findings that were reported in the *Pittsburgh Courier.* Woodard's eyeballs were pulverized, the report said, leaving only the tiniest piece of cornea in each eye, and no reaction in either. The nerve head of each had been destroyed; there was no light perception.

The report concluded, "There is absolutely no possibility of Woodard regaining his sight by the transferral of the eyes from Mr. Copeland." Instead, it was suggested that "the eyes should be cleaned out thoroughly and a gold ball placed in each socket. This would prepare him for plastic eyes."[17]

At twenty-seven years old, Woodard had been blinded for life. During the first weeks after the incident, there was little mention of it outside South Carolina. But when the NAACP's head office got involved, the story soon became a national sensation. Black newspapers across the country unleashed a torrent of outrage in their editorial pages. And Orson Welles used his radio broadcast to vent his anger in a series of blistering editorials, beginning in September and lasting through the fall of 1946.

"What does it cost to be a Negro?" Welles asked. "In Aiken, South Carolina, it cost a man his eyes. What does it cost to wear over your skeleton the pinkish tint officially described as white? In Aiken, South Carolina, it costs a man his soul." Welles would eventually correct himself and note that the blinding of the black veteran had taken place in Batesburg, but he was unapologetic in his zeal to bring to justice the men who had wielded the nightsticks. After the NAACP brought the case to his attention, he threatened to hunt down the police officer who'd blinded Woodard and spread his name over the airwaves.

"Officer X, I'm talking to you," Welles bellowed from the radio, the dramatic roar arresting in its intensity, especially by today's broadcast standards. Welles's commentaries on Isaac Woodard expressed genuine, unfiltered outrage:

> Wash your hands, Officer X, wash them well. Scrub and scully. You won't blot out the blood of a blinded war veteran. Now yet the color of your skin, your own skin, you'll never, never, never change it. Wash your hands, Officer X. Wash a lifetime, you'll never wash away that leprous lack of pigment, the guilty pallor of the White Man. We invite you to luxuriate in secrecy. It will be brief. Go on. Suck on your anonymous moment while it lasts. You're going to be uncovered. We will blast out your name. We'll give the world your given name, Officer X. Yes, and your so-called Christian name, it's going to rise out of the filthy deep like the dead thing it is. We're going to make it public with a public scandal you dictated but failed to sign.

A few weeks later, Welles made good on his promise to cast a harsh national spotlight on Shull. "I promised I'd hunt him down. I have. I gave my word. I see him unmasked. I have unmasked him. I am going to haunt Police Chief Shull for all the rest of his natural life. Mr. Shull is not going to forget me. And what's more important, I'm not going to let you forget, Mr. Shull."[18]

Welles vowed to keep that spotlight on Shull, a small-town

sheriff who worked in a building that was not much larger than a four-bedroom house:

> I'll never lose you. If they try you, I'm going to watch the trial. If they jail you, I'm going to wait for your first day of freedom. You won't be free of me. I want to see who's waiting for you at the prison gates. I want to know who will acknowledge that they know you. I'm interested in your future. I will take careful note of all your destinations; assume another name and I will be careful that the name you would forget is not forgotten. I will find means to remove from you all refuge, Officer X, you can't get rid of me. We have an appointment, you and I, and only death can cancel it.

Not the appointment but Welles's program was canceled. After Welles ignored several pleas from ABC to desist from his unyielding campaign and offended several sponsors by sympathizing with civil rights and Communist-leaning organizations, his show was pulled from the airwaves. Soon thereafter, Welles fled America for Europe, partly to escape questioning by the House Un-American Activities Committee.

But his blistering focus on the fate of Isaac Woodard led others to take up the cause: folksinger Woody Guthrie and calypso artist Lord Invader both wrote songs in the serviceman's honor. Woodard traveled the country, raising thousands of dollars for the NAACP.

Even as Welles had begun his instigation in September, NAACP executive secretary Walter White had presented the Woodard case to President Harry Truman, who'd expressed shock and dismay that South Carolina had failed to investigate the case aggressively. Within a week, at Truman's insistence, the Justice Department stepped in. Within a month, Shull and the other officer had been indicted.[19] The national outcry was so strong that even some South Carolina newspapers chastised the governor for not having conducted the investigation with greater alacrity. The case went to trial in November; after less than an hour of jury deliberation, Shull was found innocent on all charges. Spectators in the courtroom hooted and cheered. Woodard, according to news accounts, wept openly "through what remained of his shattered eyes."

Woodard went to a school for the blind in Connecticut and later moved to New York, where he used money raised in his behalf by the NAACP to purchase an apartment building. Though he aspired to become an entrepreneur, Woodard quickly fell on hard times. His wife left him, and he had a few run-ins with the law for fighting and petty theft. He lived in relative obscurity, though for weeks his blinding had been front-page news. He died on September 23, 1992, largely ignored by the media, despite the importance of his ordeal to the civil rights struggle.

Woodard's case provoked President Truman to name a commission on civil rights in December 1946, just weeks after Shull's acquittal. That commission produced the landmark report *To Secure These Rights,* which, among other things, recommended the end of segregation in the armed forces. Truman was clearly moved by the Woodard case. In a letter to his friend and fellow World War I veteran Ernest Roberts, he wrote, "When a Mayor and a City Marshal can take a Negro Sergeant off a bus in South Carolina, beat him up and put out one of his eyes, and nothing is done about it by State Authorities, something is radically wrong with the system."[20]

In another letter, this one to Charles G. Bolte, chairman of the American Veterans Committee—the group that pushed to make crimes against uniformed servicemen and servicewomen federal offenses—the president wrote, "We have only recently completed a long and bitter war against intolerance in other lands. A cruel price in blood and suffering was paid by the American people in bringing that war to a successful conclusion. Yet, in this country today there exists disturbing evidence of intolerance and prejudice similar in kind, though perhaps not in degree, to that against which we fought in the war."[21]

Nearly two years after he was presented with the Woodard case, in July 1948, and despite stiff opposition from top military officers, Truman enacted Executive Order 9981, outlawing racial discrimination in the armed forces by ensuring "equality of treatment and opportunity for all persons in the armed services without regard to race, color, religion or national origin."

From Uncle Joe I've learned that the Norris men paid close attention to all news involving blacks in the military—from the push for equal access to G.I. benefits to the violence waged against black veterans determined to secure their civil rights. They hung on every word about these matters in newspapers and on radio. My father and grandfather were big Orson Welles fans. When I was a teenager, my father made me stay at home one Sunday evening to listen to a rebroadcast of *The War of the Worlds.* While I pouted about missing some outing with my cousins, he sat riveted to the edge of his seat, as if listening to the broadcast for the first time. It is hard to imagine that he would not have heard Welles's blistering screeds against the police officer who blinded Woodard only days after he himself had been shot.

What must it have been like to pick up the paper and read about scandalous violence against black men who had fought for human rights abroad? News stories covered the murder of army veteran John C. Jones, who was tortured to death with a blowtorch and meat cleaver in Minden, Louisiana, and the shooting of army veteran George Dorsey along with his wife, sister, and brother-in-law in Monroe, Georgia. That my father's brush with Birmingham law enforcement occurred in

1946, a year when violence against black veterans raged across the land and in his own hometown, deepened the mystery of his silence about the event.

I've since spoken to black World War II veterans who, like Belvin Norris, endured slights and indignities while and after serving their country. To a man, they'd kept their stories to themselves, refusing to discuss them with their lovers or their wives, their children or coworkers or fellow church members. Tales of bitterness or victimization did not jibe with the narratives of themselves they'd created. As I delved deeper into the matter, I was consumed by anger and confusion: not only because I'd been deprived of my father's story but because the collective story of the black World War II veteran had been slighted in the popular history of the period.

Every February, when Black History Month rolls around, the country honors black achievement in newspapers and magazines, on TV shows and in schools. These tributes tend to focus on a time line that starts with slavery and fast-forwards to the mid-fifties through the mid-sixties, as if Harriet Tubman and Frederick Douglass passed the baton directly to Rosa Parks and Martin Luther King Jr. The civil rights icon Julian Bond has said that the protest for equal rights by black World War II veterans and the blinding of Isaac Woodard marked the beginning of the modern-day civil rights movement. You would hardly know it, judging from the scant attention given to these events.

The treatment of black veterans during and after World War II is a hard truth for America to embrace. Unlike the civil rights struggles of the sixties, which enshrined clear-cut heroes and villains, discrimination suffered by black veterans challenges the country's core values, the offending party being the federal government itself, which had insisted on its moral authority in the fight against xenophobia overseas. This is perhaps why Black History Month emphasizes the Martin Luther

King era—its marches, sit-ins, and protests—even as it all but ignores the earlier struggles of men and women who worked hard to underscore the country's untenable moral contradiction. The story of these men and women instances a special brand of grace: they had every reason to stoke their anger at America but chose instead to seek a higher ground. While they hoped for and, in some cases, demanded the right to vote, fair wages, and equal housing, they were also asserting a much more basic claim. They wanted the right simply to be ordinary: to be able to walk into a Woolworth's, order a ham sandwich, and savor it on the spot; to be able to fly a kite with a son or daughter anywhere in a park without fear of retribution; to be able to pass a white woman on the street without her trampling on their pride by clutching her pocketbook a little closer or, worse, threatening their lives by crying disrespect.

Chances are you've encountered these veterans, men and women, at work or church or Walmart without knowing it. And probably, like me before I started writing this book, you knew little if anything about their sacrifices and triumphs in the quest for a better America.

On the frigid Tuesday morning of Inauguration Day 2009, old black men in uniform made their way to Washington, D.C., to witness the nation's first black president, the commander in chief, taking the oath of office. Many were clutching old photographs of themselves and others during their service, or had pictures in small frames or encased in plastic, taped or pinned to their lapels or winter hats. I hosted National Public Radio's live coverage that day with my colleague Steve Inskeep. I usually host in the afternoon, but on that day I had to keep Steve's early morning hours. At 4:45 a.m. on January 20, I encountered a stooped old man in a tan triangular army hat on Massachusetts Avenue. He was inching, slow as molasses, on his way to the Capitol, but he lifted himself upright and leaned against a younger man who could have been his son to salute me as I passed. "I can barely walk, but I am going to be standing proud today," he said, his words punctuated by puffs of condensation in the predawn cold. "Stand all day if I have to, to see this."

I wondered if he was actually going to make it to the Capitol grounds to see the ceremony, not only because he moved so slowly but because he seemed to pause and salute almost every person he met on the street. The distance that stooped old gentleman had already traveled had once been unimaginable: from when, as a young man, he first put on his army cap to this morning, when he pulled it over his now graying hair to watch a black man raise his hand to take the oath of office as president of the United States. Eric Holder, soon to become the attorney general, told me that all day he harbored thoughts of his father, an immigrant from Barbados who fiercely loved the United States and fought in the war but who, on his way home, had to stand for hours on end during his train ride, while German prisoners of war, all white men, sat comfortably in cushioned seats.

January 20, by tradition, is the day American presidents take the oath of office. January 20, 1946, was my father's last full day in the navy; he was discharged on the following morning. I, too, thought of my father on Inauguration Day, wondering what he would have made of the ascension of a black president of the United States, a black commander in chief. The answer brought tears to my eyes.

11

A Date with Justice

THE MAN ACCUSED OF BLINDING Isaac Woodard, Police Chief Lynwood Shull, pretty much disappeared from the historical record after his acquittal in November 1946. He stayed in and around Batesburg for most of his life. He had a daughter and worked for a time as the county road commissioner. He died in December 1997, at the age of ninety-five. Eager to know more about him, I called up some of his relatives: not a one had a clue that Lynwood Shull had been a figure in the national news for his involvement in the Woodard case. They had no idea that Shull had been the subject of a series of radio tirades by Orson Welles, the creator of *Citizen Kane* and *The War of the Worlds.* Most were dumbfounded to discover that their relative had been accused of a crime so heinous as to prompt executive action by a sitting U.S. president. Some were eager to get me off the phone, but others wanted to hear more.

Patsy Quarles, who married into the family, learned of the story from news clippings she discovered while cleaning out her in-laws' farmstead. "It was hush-hush," she said. "I was married thirty years before I even heard it mentioned. At that time a newspaper article turned up and I said what was this about and [my husband] said it is not something the family talks about." Quarles told me that she wants to know more but is afraid to press the subject.

Hugh Shull, who lives in Lexington, South Carolina, is a nephew of Shull's. His father, Cothran, was the youngest of the six Shull siblings; Lynwood was the oldest. When I asked

Hugh if he had ever heard of Isaac Woodard, he said, "Never heard a word of any of this, and I am fifty-seven years old." In one of the most uncomfortable conversations I've been party to, I read Woodard's affidavit to Hugh Shull on the phone; he gasped time and again at the other end of the line.

"He is my uncle Lynwood," Hugh Shull said. "It is a shock to me. Yes, ma'am. Not so much a shock that things like that happened in that period. But a shock that he would do that." I explained that my father was a black veteran also wounded in a police shooting, and that he, too, had kept the story to himself to avoid passing his pain on to his loved ones. Shull told me, "They say that was the greatest generation, the ability to try to protect their family, and I guess that is what they did. They protected their families." The Shull family had also been burdened, it appears, and in some way shaped, by the weight of silence. Hugh Shull seemed conflicted about what he'd heard. "It makes me feel ashamed that something like that happened, and I don't know if I should apologize or what, but I just don't want to talk about it anymore."

Davis and Betty Shull live in nearby Aiken County, South Carolina. They were not close to Lynwood Shull; they last saw him at a livestock market years before his death. They, too, were in the dark about Lynwood, but, as they see it, the connection of their family name to the Woodard scandal is no cause for apology. "It does not bother me," Davis Shull, Lynwood's cousin, said. "I did not know it. I would assume the man could have been at fault. If he [Shull] was acquitted, [Woodard] probably did something."

Davis Shull is troubled by the notion that all Shulls—all southerners, for that matter—should be besmirched by any one incident. "We're all supposed to be haters," Davis said. "But hey! We have relatives who are black. We know who they are. Goes back to my great-granddaddy. We knew who they are and one of them was even raised up in the same house with my grandmother. In some ways we see things more clearly." His wife, Betty, noted that the South's tortured history vis-à-vis race makes it hard for whites to wade into racial discussions. "Nowadays everything is racist," she told me. "No matter what you say. You can't tell the truth without being racist. You can't say anything."

Listening to Davis and Betty Shull, I couldn't help but think of the newsreels from the civil rights era's most vicious conflicts. Lynwood Shull is dead, but many of the people who threw bricks at college students, or spat at ballplayers, or yelled awful things at schoolchildren are still alive. And if America is as determined as it appears to be to have a frank conversation about race, these very people, who've been denounced and derided—demonized—must have a seat at the table, so that they can be a part of that dialogue. For often discussions about race are one-sided, driven only by those who have experienced directly or through family ties the burden of rampant and vicious discrimination. The "success despite oppression" trope is quite common in politics, business, and the media. Less common—more muted, perhaps—are the viewpoints of people who enforced, enjoyed, or evolved past presumed white privilege. Their stories and sentiments, too, must be considered for greater understanding, as all of us try to explore and explain a country that has moved from the legislated marginalization of people of color to their predicted attainment of majority status in less than forty years.

It was my need to hear from the other side, as it were, that spurred my quest: to search out either the policemen involved in Belvin Norris's shooting or their relatives. From the police docket and the court records, I knew the names of the officers. I knew what they looked like, having examined their faces in Alabama law enforcement convention programs. I knew what they wore to work: a shiny dark uniform, with a gold-colored badge affixed. I knew where they lived in 1946. I knew their wives' names. And, with not as much success as I had hoped, I tried to track down their children as well as distant family members because, while I was obsessed with piecing my father's story together, I also needed to know as much as possible about who these policemen were as human beings and what they told their children, if anything at all, about that fateful February night—fateful, at least, for me and my family. I would encounter mostly dead ends and death notices. All five men involved in the incident had passed way.

Bradley Pate, Carl Baggett, and Tremon Lindsey were married to women with names that seemed to spring from southern popular fiction. Names that adorned a lady like a brooch or a bouquet. Zelphia. Aleen. Ruby. Even though the policemen's families had lived on the opposite side of the color line, I was surprised by how similar their lives were to the Birmingham Norrises'. Carl Baggett, for instance, lived on Avenue Z in Ensley, not far from my grandparents' house. George Neil, who died in Florida in 1967, was one of six sons, like the Norris brothers. The officers had moved to Birmingham from rural areas and lived in squat one-story wooden bungalows on the West or South Side, most of which, like my grandparents' house, have since been torn down.

They were older men who'd stayed behind in Birmingham while thousands of youth headed off to war. They worked for a police department riddled with corruption and subject to derision. A detailed examination of the department by the Birmingham Citizen's Committee found that the four-hundred-member force suffered from "impaired morals" in the late forties and early fifties, partly because large companies like the steel giant TCI had their own police unit and tended to siphon off the most qualified applicants with better pay and benefits. Starting pay for a Birmingham police officer was $259.88 per month, slightly less than what could be earned in the mills or the mines.

The men were required to provide their own flashlights and pistols. The resulting motley array of firearms confused ballistic analysis whenever officers were involved in a shooting. New police recruits often got their pistols from pawnbrokers, which is to say that firearms used by criminals could easily wind up in police holsters. And when policemen got their guns through conventional retailers, they often used money borrowed from loan sharks, a practice that the Citizen's Committee understandably found troubling, noting, "We see the possibility of serious detriment to the service when young officers are forced into such contracts." The Citizen's Committee's investigation of the Birmingham police concluded that "most of the force are decent, well meaning men who earnestly try to be fair and considerate in the discharge of their duties"; but they also determined that its leadership left much to be desired. Bull Connor, then a thin man with slicked-back hair and a salty tongue, was sternly criticized. He was rated as "deficient in executive ability" and charged with practicing favoritism.[1]

Of the five officers involved in Belvin Norris's shooting, so far as I know, two left the force early to pursue other work. George Neil moved to Panama City, Florida, where he became the city clerk. Detective Macon Espy moved to Joplin, Missouri, to work for a company that hauled dynamite, and later ran a motel with his wife in Gulf Shores, Alabama. Espy had a notorious career as a policeman. In 1940, he was mentioned in a "Goofy Gazette" newspaper column for having served his own wife, Eleanor, a warrant for reckless driving. And in 1948 he was suspended from duty for thirty days; it appeared that a handcuffed suspect he was driving from Greensboro, North Carolina, to Birmingham had managed to reach over to the front seat and snag Espy's pistol sixty miles or so outside Birmingham.

Espy's sister-in-law Betty Koonce is one of the few relatives directly connected to the officers who was willing to talk. In her eighties, she still lives in Birmingham and describes herself as the "sole survivor" of her family. Betty remembers when William Macon Espy started courting her older sister, Eleanor. Once married, they lived in a house next to her parents'. He was a simple man, she said. Not very tall and not a real talker. He liked straw hats and fiddle music. And, Betty said, he was a good friend of Bull Connor's, one of "Bull's boys." He'd get a call from Bull, she recalled, and he would be off running at all hours of the night.

As was to be expected, Espy never mentioned a shooting involving young black men in a downtown Birmingham office building, Koonce said. He never talked about his work at home, period. Betty Koonce did remember reading about him in the paper once. She was fuzzy about the details but recollected that the item involved a shooting at the courthouse. Indeed, in 1938 the *Birmingham News* carried a story about a shooting: a thirty-five-year-old salesman named H. E. Coburn shot a "negro" being escorted through the Birmingham courthouse by Espy, shortly after the "negro" was convicted of a crime against Coburn's daughter.

From Betty Koonce I learned little of factual relevance about the Birmingham police officers who'd confronted my father in the Pythian Temple, but from what she said I was able to etch the arc of their lives. My conversation with her and other relatives helped me to understand segregation from the other side of Birmingham's color line.

Betty has seen a lot of changes in her life and was at first reluctant to talk about the role of the Birmingham police during the push for racial equality. She referred to it as "the unpleasantness," revealing discomfort about discussing America's version of apartheid. "It always makes us look so bad, but it is just the way it was," she said. "You know, we didn't know anything else."

"I am from the old school," she added. "I had to accept these blacks as my next-door neighbors. It used to be easier. Back then, we had our own. But you know things changed, and some of the best friends I ever had were black. I don't have anything against them, only the ones who are snooty or trying to prove themselves."

I asked Betty to clarify what she meant by the ones who are trying to prove themselves. "It is still a shock for me to pick up a paper for the last year and see that a black man is a leader of this country. . . . I just can't get used to it. But they have accepted it. The people I never thought would stand for it have accepted it. You can't stand in the way of progress."

It's what she wants to believe, and she does, but she also has an inkling of a reservation that she just can't shake. "I have a gut feeling—and I have had it for a while—when they brought up Obama, I thought, 'Oh me! Some of those rednecks are going to get their sights on him.' I have a feeling that boy better watch his back because someone is going to put their sights on him." When I asked her to be more expansive, she told me, "I've said enough." To make sure I got the point, she added: "No more!"

I still wanted to know more about the role police officers played in Jim Crow Birmingham. The Citizen's Committee report suggests that Birmingham's police department was defined by Bull Connor's rough-and-tumble leadership long before the 1960s. What is not clear is whether all the men under his command subscribed to his politics or his tactics. After realizing I would never be able to confront any of the policemen involved in my father's shooting, I turned to someone who knew more than a thing or two about the Birmingham police force in the 1940s.

On a hot July afternoon I sought Justice—Aubrey Justice,

one of the very few forties-era policemen still residing in Birmingham. For a time, his partner on the squad had been a patrolman whose last name was Crook. Crook and Justice. No kidding. When I flew to Birmingham to meet Aubrey Justice, I stopped at the rental-car counter, where the women at the desk greeted me like an old friend. "Here on business again?" "Yes, ma'am," I said almost instinctively. Funny, how I tend to slip into southern niceties only minutes after stepping foot on red clay. "I can give you an upgrade," she said. "Something you might like." Since I'd booked a budget rate, any upgrade would likely offer more legroom and perhaps windows you didn't have to roll down by hand. But I stiffened when she perused the list of available rental vehicles and pointed to a racy Mustang. "It's a red one," she said. "Candy-apple red. Very sleek." And ostentatious. Testosterone on wheels. I heard my father talking to me.

During summer visits to Birmingham, whenever we left Grandma's house in Ensley to go downtown, he would say, "Don't call attention to yourself. Don't be loud or rambunctious." As we got old enough to care about our outward appearance (the moment, Grandma said, we'd start to "smell ourselves"), he would add, "There's nothing wrong with being proud. You just have to know the difference between being proud and being highfalutin."

I took the keys to the candy-apple red, highfalutin, powerful driving machine and daydreamed about Dad as I rolled through English Village and then on to Mountain Brook, the toniest neighborhood in Birmingham. As I drove through these streets, I was struck by how inconceivable this ride would have been during my visits to Birmingham in the 1960s and 1970s. I was now headed for Crestline Village, a neighborhood of neat homes and aggressively landscaped yards, just down the hill from the Mountain Brook mansions where Birmingham's corporate titans raise their families. Real estate agents in Crestline refer to the area as "Mountain Brook–adjacent." Aubrey Justice lives in a crisp white Cape Cod–style home surrounded by well-tended perennials. As I exited the car and walked to the front door, I had the feeling my every step was being watched.

I should have listened to Dad's voice; the Mustang had been an impulsive but foolish choice. A simple sedan, such as the one in Justice's driveway, would have been more appropriate. I thought of what Mom would have said: "Well, you know why she offered you that fancy car? She thinks black people can't help themselves when it comes to fancy cars. I'm surprised she didn't offer you an upgrade to a Cadillac. You should have taught her a lesson about our values by choosing something suitable instead of stylish."

Mom's imagined advice suffused me with warmth, the comfort I'd feel in grade school when I'd find a note from her in my lunch box, telling me to use my nickel to buy regular instead of chocolate milk. The memory put me at ease as I stepped up to ring the doorbell. Aubrey Justice must have had his eyes on me, for he was at the front door in a flash. When he opened the screen door I sensed that he, too, assumed unwanted spectators. He looked past me toward the street, furtively glancing this way and that to see if a neighbor had spotted the stranger at his house. He waved to a fellow mowing his lawn down the street and chuckled to himself before ushering me in.

I liked him immediately.

We chatted in his living room, where he sat in what appeared to be his favorite chair, an overstuffed brown lounger. It was one of a pair separated by a table with a crystal lamp. At the base of each lounger was a half-moon rug. There was something sweet about these his-and-hers recliners, where Aubrey and Wadean Justice spend their evenings watching a huge flat-screen TV—a recent upgrade so large that it crowds the carefully arranged vintage children's photos displayed on a shared wall.

Aubrey Justice is handsome in a Spencer Tracy sort of way: White hair. Sparkling blue eyes. Deep tan. A few dark patches on his arms betray how much time he's spent in the sun. He limps ever so slightly, one foot turning inward when he walks. Yet his skin is taut and his movements sharp. He's an avid golfer and a good one. He had just celebrated his birthday on the links, where he'd shot a 69.

Justice was originally from a rural area in Shelby County. After the war, he moved to Birmingham, where he worked as a laborer for American Bridge before enrolling in the police academy. He was a beat cop and spent much of his time patrolling the seedier fringes of Birmingham's black business district, an area called the "scratch-ankle district." The name derives from either a dance style or the aggressive red ants that might scamper up your leg in barrooms and brothels with dirt floors.

Justice joined the force in 1949, after returning from service in the war as an army paratrooper. To lighten the mood, I asked if his name had led him to a career in law enforcement. "Naw," he replied. "I just decided that I wanted to. Went down and took the civil service test and they hired me. Simple as that."

Since police officers didn't make much money, he usually worked two jobs, moonlighting at nightclubs until he'd had enough of the nightly coal miners' fistfights. "I finally got tired of that," he told me. "I said, I'm tired of this blood money, so I got me a job working at a driving range, giving golf lessons and everything." He carefully managed his dual responsibilities: to remain in good stead as a police officer, he avoided rocking the boat even when he questioned the way Connor ran the department. "We all didn't think like Bull Connor though, but we had to do a certain amount of orders because [it was] either that or get fired, but we said we had families and we couldn't do anything but do what we had to do."

I asked Justice how difficult it was to work for Bull Connor if you didn't share Connor's belief in strict segregation, and he explained that officers had to be shrewd. "Well, you had ways to get around things," he said. "I mean, you had to . . . certain things you had to do, some things you might not like. But you had to do it 'cause it's either that or get fired." As to what the "certain things you had to do" were, he refused to say. To hear him tell it, relations between police officers and blacks in the city were "fine." "We didn't have no problems at all," he insisted. "Everybody knew their place."

Justice is a guarded storyteller. He was careful not to reveal too much about his time in a police department that's been judged through the harsh lens of history. He was more willing to talk about the subjects he encountered during street patrols than the officers he worked with. I noticed that he had a certain fondness for the ne'er-do-wells he described, the men who ran the juke joints or sold moonshine on the sly to policemen. You'd think he was talking about an old chum when he described a police informant who drank paint thinner when he couldn't afford liquor. They were all black and described by Justice as decent fellows who lacked the wherewithal to make an honest living. Nowhere in Aubrey's stories were any black men I recognized. Working men. Family men. Churchgoing, mortgage-paying, lawn-mowing, upright-till-the-day-they-die kind of men. Perhaps the strict color line prevented contact between the white Birmingham police and ordinary black men, or perhaps ordinary black men went to pains to steer clear of the police.

By the 1960s, Aubrey Justice, like most of Birmingham, found himself amid the convulsion of civil rights protests, when residential bombings becoming so frequent that Birmingham was called "Bombingham." It was hard for Justice not to be front and center at some seminal events in Birmingham's civil rights history. While administering a sobriety test to a suspected drunk driver in the city jail one day, he heard peals of laughter down the hall. He turned to see a group of officers—

some in uniform, some in street clothes—bringing Martin Luther King to jail. "As far as I could see, they did not mistreat him. They were just joking and cutting up and carrying on," he related. Was King, too, laughing and joking? "I don't think he had any ill feelings toward them, you know," Aubrey said. Police in Birmingham knew all too well that King's and the Southern Christian Leadership Conference's nonviolent tactics were intended to provoke arrests for greater publicity.

Aubrey Justice also saw his share of violence. He was one of the police officers assigned to guard the home of civil rights attorney Arthur Shores, after it had been firebombed twice within one month. He was also summoned to guard the home of activist Fred Shuttlesworth, after someone put sticks of dynamite under his bedroom window. Shuttlesworth has maintained that a police officer invoked the Ku Klux Klan shortly after the bombing and warned him to "get out of town." In these times the Birmingham Police Department was racked by tension and, in some cases, conflicting loyalties. Some officers didn't hide their Klan sympathies. For his part, Justice said, he "wasn't in favor of committing crimes against anybody . . . I think there were some bad ones there. But I also know there was a lot of dedicated good, good people there. You go to church and you find all kinds of different people. Good ones. Bad ones. Go to the police department, find good ones. Bad ones. That's just the way life was."

On Sunday September 15, 1963, Justice was assigned to traffic duty in the East Lake district. The day was overcast and unseasonably cold. At about half past ten that morning, his patrol radio crackled with orders to get downtown to Sixteenth Street as fast as possible. Justice was one of the first officers to arrive on the scene after nineteen sticks of dynamite had ripped through the Sixteenth Street Baptist Church, a rallying site for the civil rights movement. The dynamite, which all but destroyed the church, had been placed near the basement, where children had gathered to change into their church robes after Sunday school. The sermon that day was supposed to be "The Love That Forgives." The church clock is still frozen at 10:22 a.m.

As Aubrey Justice tells it, while he didn't hear the blast, he did hear the shrill wail of sirens as he got closer to the bombed sanctuary. The streets were crowded. There were cries and shouts. Dazed churchgoers mired by concrete dust shared the street with young onlookers roused from bed by the explosion, now demanding retribution. There was no doubt that there would be casualties, but in those first moments, Justice said, no one yet knew that four little girls had perished, or that twenty had been badly injured. "It was so crowded and so bad that we had to make them all get in a house," Justice said. As to how exactly this was achieved, he only allowed, "Let's just say we made them get into a house."

Justice busied himself directing traffic, trying, along with other officers, to disperse the crowd as much as possible and prevent anyone from heading toward the scene of devastation. As it happened, some of the people turned away were parents of the slain little girls; they'd dropped their daughters off for Sunday school and had returned for Sunday service. That day Aubrey got home bedraggled and discomfited: he and his wife, Wadean, knew that race relations in Birmingham would never be the same.

After spending a few hours with Aubrey Justice, I was touched by something I didn't fully understand at the time. Only later, upon reflection on his life and our conversation, did it occur to me that I'd been sitting knee to knee with an older white man who was in odd ways a mirror image of the black man who'd raised me. At first I pushed the thought away. For myriad reasons, I didn't want to go there. Segregation was informed by, and sought to keep alive, the illusion that white and black people are fundamentally different, one superior to the other. But the illusion could sometimes work both ways, for many blacks have refused to see anything of themselves in their oppressors, the race responsible for their denigration.

Maybe it was all that talk about golf and Justice's well-tended garden. Or maybe it was the big brown recliner, where Aubrey said he often fell asleep. Similarities between Aubrey Justice and Belvin Norris kept creeping up on me. The two men were born one year apart. Dad graduated from high school in 1943, Justice in '44. Both had gone off to war; both had been headed to Japan when the war came to a close, after bombs fell on Hiroshima and Nagasaki. To be sure, in the armed services Justice had had opportunities that were denied my father; unlike Belvin, he had not been demeaned because of the color of his skin. As a paratrooper, he had benefited from a higher pay grade. It also turned out that, for all their obvious differences, Aubrey and Belvin held similar views about the tactics used by civil rights advocates in the 1950s and '60s.

In May 1963, Justice had not been among the police officers in Kelly Ingram Park who unleashed dogs on peaceful demonstrators while firemen turned hoses on schoolchildren, but he does have a clear memory and sharp opinions about what happened that day.

"I thought the whole thing was nothing but a show. Nothing happened till they'd all gathered down there and they'd be standing and wouldn't do nothing. And the minute the police got there, they'd start and they'd egg them dogs on, and this and that and the other, and it was just a mess. They knew it was going to happen." According to Justice, the protesters were intent on getting arrested to incur sympathy, to persuade others of the rightness of their cause.

I'd heard all that before. My father had great respect for Martin Luther King. He wept an ocean when King died and kept his image in his locker at the post office. Even so, he was uncomfortable when civil rights leaders who had not been born and raised in Birmingham became leaders in Birmingham's civil rights struggles. He referred to them as "that Atlanta crowd." And when newsmen would describe Birmingham as "the most segregated city in America," he'd grouse at the TV: "What? Did they hold a contest?" While Birmingham may have broken his heart, it still had a strong hold on him, despite his need to flee the city. The actuality and portrayal of his hometown as a racial Armageddon pained him, perhaps because of a mixture of pride and guilt. After all, his aging parents still had to walk the streets where blood had been shed. And he must have worried that residents and businesses would abandon the city to escape chaos or stigma, resulting in its demise.

Justice, too, worried about the city's image, as well as the police department's reputation, after shocking pictures documenting the confrontations at Kelly Ingram Park were beamed around the world. "Seemed to me," he said, "like what they should have done [is] just let them go ahead and protest as long as they didn't damage anything or tear up anything or do anything. Of course, I wasn't involved."

At the time, Justice thought that what happened in that park would amplify black hatred of the police, casting a grim shadow over all of Birmingham. He was right. Bull Connor was forced from office in May 1963, and ever since the police department and politicians have worked hard to repair Birmingham's badly damaged image. Yet, regarding the scandal of Kelly Ingram Park, John F. Kennedy remarked, "The civil rights movement should thank God for Bull Connor. He's helped it as much as Abraham Lincoln."

Aubrey Justice and my father had one more thing in common: both were assaulted across the color line. By the mid-seventies, Justice increasingly found himself working at police headquarters. One Thanksgiving weekend, he was fulfilling his duties as desk sergeant when a young black man approached him about some stolen property. The man gave Justice a description and an address. Justice turned his back to consult the docket; when he turned around to face the complainant, a different young black man was standing there, pointing a gun through an opening in the glass partition.

The young man pulled the trigger. Justice remembers the click. The gun was either jammed or not loaded. His eyes were tightly shut until he realized he was still alive and uninjured. He saw the youth scramble down the stairs and out the front door, yelling, "Kill the pigs!" Justice flew into the radio room to tell all officers in the vicinity to be on the lookout for the culprit. But there was a problem: he couldn't remember what the young man looked like. Only the nickel-plated pistol. He couldn't recall if the assailant was short or tall, thin or fat, light- or dark-skinned. Nothing.

Though Justice had been sharing robust tales with me for hours, his voice got reedy when discussing the attempt on his life. "I just couldn't identify him," he sighed. His fellow police officers showed Justice mug shots and collared possible suspects, to no avail. I asked Justice if he was under pressure to identify someone. "I wanted to identify someone," he said. But he felt he had to be sure of the thug's identity. For Justice wondered, "What would happen if they caught him? And what if it was the wrong kid?" Indeed.

Justice said he tried hard to set the incident aside, to reject the instinct to demonize all black people as a result of one man's criminality. He fully embraces integration in the workplace and in his neighborhood; he is empathetic with regard to his adult children's friendship with blacks. But still he harbors a certain nostalgia for bygone days.

"Everyone should have certain rights," he told me. "It's just that we was raised to be separate, and I felt like maybe probably we ought to live separate." Justice said society had to get past that point of view but that in doing so, something was lost:

"In some ways it seems like things were better when the races had their own."

Now, I know I am supposed to be offended by Aubrey's remarks. But after spending time in Alabama digging into my father's past, I wonder whether Justice might not be speaking the truth, at least in part. You can't visit my grandparents' street in Ensley and avoid asking, Did integration work as planned? You can't go back to Parker High—once Birmingham's only high school for blacks—and not ponder if desegregation created a tide that lifted some blacks, but also an undertow that pulled others deeper into poverty and isolation.

A. H. Parker High School had been mythic when I was growing up. As a member of the blue-jeans-and-sneakers generation, I would look with heightened curiosity at vintage pictures from Parker in our family collection. The girls wore dresses. The boys sported skinny ties and starched white shirts. Dress codes were strict. "Dress for success" had apparently been the mantra. Though I was serious about schooling, embracing it as a responsibility, my attitude was a far cry from the passion my father and his brothers had for Parker. I know people who have such fierce allegiances to their alma maters. I am married to a man who is fanatical about the University of Michigan. But I have never seen such severe, misty-eyed loyalty to a high school. For them, Parker was a symbol of pride; it showed the outside world that blacks could prosper against all odds.

Fred Horn, one of my father's classmates, served sixteen years as a state legislator. He later taught at the school. He coached basketball, golf, and football and was the primary force behind the establishment of the athletic field behind the school that now bears his name. "We believed that we were better than anybody else," Horn said. "This was taught. And we had to graduate and prove to ourselves and to the world that we were better."

Nearly all the students who served as foot soldiers for freedom in the 1963 protest came from Parker High School. Hundreds of children walked the few blocks from Parker to the Sixteenth Street Baptist Church, where Dr. Martin Luther King had told them to march with pride and without violence. These students were then attacked by dogs and with water cannons. Timothy Archie was at Kelly Ingram Park that afternoon. He said the force of a water cannon sent him flying as though he were "a piece of paper." He was bruised for weeks, but has no regrets. "This was the turning point of the civil right movement here in Birmingham," he told me. "Children made the change. We made the change."

At Parker High School nowadays, it is hard to argue that, on the whole, change was for the better. The school sits in the shadows of the city's downtown, but it might as well be a galaxy away. It is surrounded by sagging bungalows and boarded-up buildings. The campus, once so lovingly maintained that it was featured on postcards sold in stores throughout the city, now abounds with weeds, trash, and graffiti.

Under segregation, Parker was a place where the children of black doctors and ditchdiggers learned side by side. Under integration, the best and the brightest moved to better-equipped schools elsewhere in the city and the suburbs. Today Parker is still 98 percent black, but because the black middle class has fled, there's de facto segregation based on class, not color. On college entrance exams, students at Parker now perform well below the national average, so much so that the state has threatened to intervene.

When I went back to Parker on a reporting trip in 2004, I was stunned to see that Dad's likeness was on a wall in the lunchroom. They didn't have yearbooks back then, just class photos—hundreds of tiny oval portraits on a single eleven-by-fourteen-inch sheet of paper. Of all the Parker graduating classes, the sheet including Belvin and Woody Norris had been blown up and affixed to a large wall, like a vintage mural. The Norris brothers graduated the same year, 1943. Now, together with hundreds of others in suits and ties and neat dresses, they look out from that mural over students who wear hoodies and gold "grills" on their teeth. A few feet from the wall, a student told me, "It's still a struggle 'cause you know how they had separate but equal? It's separate but unequal, and it's still like that. I mean, despite the struggles of, you know, our forefathers in the civil rights movement, it's not separate and equal."

After leaving Parker, I went a few blocks down the road to visit former civil rights activist James Armstrong, who'd been arrested and jailed half a dozen times for his efforts. He was at the head of the Selma-to-Montgomery voting rights march in 1965 and has since carried the American flag in reenactments, year after year. Armstrong also filed the lawsuit that eventually led to the integration of Birmingham's schools, resulting in the diminishment of his very own neighborhood.

For more than fifty years he ran a barbershop near Parker. The walls inside provided a history lesson to young customers, who patronized the shop for haircuts from "back in the day": side parts, freedom 'fros, and fades. On the walls of his establishment were signs for colored restrooms and for separate entrances to movie theaters, as well as campaign posters for Jesse Jackson's presidential run and for Birmingham's first black mayor, Richard Arrington. At the entrance was a placard Armstrong had made with the city's youths in mind: IF YOU THINK EDUCATION IS EXPENSIVE, TRY IGNORANCE.

Customers had ample time to read the placard while James Armstrong slowly made his way to the front door. You see, visitors to his barbershop had to ring for service. The neighborhood had gotten so bad that Armstrong spent his days behind a locked door, a civil rights warrior living in fear. "I keep that door locked when I'm here by myself. I'm afraid of my own folks," he told me.

James Armstrong died in November 2009, at the age of eighty-six. He lived to see the struggle for civil rights sublimed by the election of Barack Obama—he'd counted himself among the longest line of black voters Birmingham had ever seen. Armstrong said he hoped that those left behind by integration would stoke the consciences of those propelled by it. I hope he's right.

At first glance, you might think that poverty is the chief vicissitude bedeviling the neighborhood around Parker or the neighborhood a few miles away where my grandparents lived. You'd be wrong. People have always been poor here. But years ago, they were also rich with social capital. There was an abiding sense of community. Every household had a breadwinner, sometimes three or four, working at the mills, the mines, the railroads, the schools. Or at the homes across town, as maids, nannies, and gardeners. Stable families were the norm. Two parents. Lots of children. Small houses. Big dreams.

Today, these black neighborhoods are composed of crumbling buildings full of people even at the height of the business day: too few adults hold jobs; too many students skip school or drop out altogether. Avenue G is no longer a supposedly poor enclave. It is unquestionably destitute—a place of broken windows and shattered dreams. Scary dogs roam with abandon. Drug dealers seem unafraid of hawking their wares in broad daylight.

My grandparents' bungalow is gone. The lot is empty; all that remains are two trees along the boulevard. In the distance I hear an ice cream truck and I'm back in 1960-something, when my grandfather would make us recite a poem or a psalm to "earn" our ice cream money. I lean against my car, listening to a

Scott Joplin rag blaring from a speaker on top of the Good Humor truck. A teenager, holding a Dreamsicle, passes me by on his bicycle. After he's halfway down the block, he turns back: "You need help? You from around here?"

I tell him my grandparents raised six boys in a house that sat on the empty lot before our eyes. The kid shrugs his shoulders. "Don't know 'em," he said. "But I tell you what. You don't need to be here. Too dangerous. You just can't roll up in this neighborhood for sightseeing. You likely to get robbed or even killed. Best you get yourself back to where you came from."

12

Home

A COIN TOSS LED BELVIN NORRIS, a man who didn't leave much to chance, to Minnesota, the place he would call home until his death.

Once Belvin and Woody Norris made their court appearance and paid their fines as recompense for their arrest, following their violent encounter with the Birmingham police, they left the state in a hurry. Birmingham was a dangerous place for black men perceived as agitators. Woody and Belvin had little money and no clear plans. One by one, their older brothers had moved to Chicago's South Side, while dozens of their classmates had hightailed it to Detroit, looking for jobs in the auto industry. But Belvin and Woody decided to head somewhere else, in part because they feared that the long arm of Alabama law enforcement might find and harass them if they followed the traditional routes of black migration north from Birmingham.

Paranoia? By today's standards, their panic might seem absurd, but in the mid-1940s southern police departments would often inform their northern counterparts about potential troublemakers, recent black arrivals in need of close monitoring. Some blacks were gripped by irrational fear of the dogged persistence of southern authorities to keep them in check, even after they'd left the region. Such was the psychological terrorism of the Jim Crow system.

Horace Huntley, who directs the Oral History Project at the Birmingham Civil Rights Institute, shook his head and shuddered as he recalled a deeply ingrained angst. Decades ago Huntley was in the military, stationed at Grand Forks, North Dakota, and during weekends he would take quick trips north to Winnipeg. "The guys had told me how liberal Canada was," Huntley said, laughing at the comedy of an encounter in retrospect. "So the first time I went to Winnipeg, Manitoba, I got on the bus. I had sat on the front seat, and about, I guess, maybe a block and a half later, a young white woman got on the bus and sat next to me. . . . Now, here I am a young black teenager, eighteen years old, from Birmingham, Alabama, never known anything different, and here this white woman was going to sit down next to me. It nearly scared me to death for a very brief period. 'Cause all I could imagine was that Bull Connor had a camera and it was on me and it was sending all this back. . . . And then, she not only sat there, she started a conversation. It's the first time I'd ever talked to a white woman or a white girl my age. And it was, it was rather traumatic . . . the trauma of growing up in apartheid Birmingham."

Woody and Belvin left the city they'd grown up in and made their way to Boston, where Dad knew someone from his years in the military. But things didn't work out well. Dad's friend had moved away by the time they arrived. They had no place to live, no work, no leads or relatives. At their wits' end, they turned once again to their older brother Simpson, and it could not have been an easy call to make. Simpson had bailed his brothers out of jail after the shooting and the arrest. Here they were again, palms out, begging for train fare to join the rest of the Norris clan in Chicago.

Soon Dad was earning decent money at a post office there. All that studying during the voter drive had been put to good use when he'd applied for a postal job and aced the civil service exam. One of his best friends at the time was a fellow postal worker named Jimmy Brown, although theirs was an unlikely friendship. Jimmy was a looker. Because of his chiseled cheekbones and carefully tended mustache, women used to tell him that he could have been Clark Gable's black brother. Jimmy liked to hang out on the town and ran with a bunch of Chicago hipsters. Belvin offered something different. "You could just trust him," Jimmy said. "He was not into all that jive talk and all that kind of stuff. He had a different way about him. You could trust him. In a fast town like Chicago, you hold on to people you can trust."

Though the Norris brothers all lived together in Chicago, Belvin and Woody were always a pair. Their childhood bond remained strong, and had perhaps been deepened by their terrifying arrest and incarceration. The pair would become a trio: Belvin, Woody, and Jimmy. Every year after Christmas, they would spend some of their overtime pay on a road trip, usually of short duration, to places throughout the Midwest, like Wisconsin Dells, Detroit, or fishing resorts in Minnesota.

Occasionally, at Belvin and Woody's behest, they would drive down to Alabama. Jimmy would go reluctantly, and only because he'd been outnumbered in the voting. Jimmy Brown was from Minneapolis and didn't much care for the South and its strict covenants. So when the time came for their next adventure, he suggested they flip a coin: heads, we go to Minnesota; tails, we go to Birmingham.

Belvin and Woody were so peeved about losing the coin toss that Jimmy was forced to be the sole driver on the eight-hour trip to the Twin Cities. The Norris brothers were still sprawled out on the backseat when Jimmy pulled off the interstate and noticed there was a dance in progress at the Labor Temple in southeast Minneapolis.

Jimmy woke them up and found a decent gas station so they could all fix themselves up a bit before going to the dance hall. "Once they got inside, you could have flown an airplane into their mouths," Jimmy said. "It was a mostly white crowd, and they just were not used to that. You know, seeing mixed couples on the dance floor and whatnot. The girls came up to them and were so nice and so talkative. They didn't know what to do. They were so shy. It tickled me." As for the white men at the dance, they treated Woody and Belvin as equals. They looked them in the eye. They waved them toward the bar and extended "you first" courtesies. This behavior by white men was unfamiliar to the brothers, but quite welcome.

So entranced were Belvin and Woody by this newness that Chicago's allure began to diminish. Belvin and Woody started visiting Minnesota regularly. Woody would eventually marry a small-town, white Minnesota girl named Audrey, who already had a young daughter. Audrey's family was at first unsettled by the union but soon came to respect Woody's charms.

As things turned out, Dad, too, would marry a Minnesotan. In 1960, Jimmy Brown's best friend became his brother-in-law. Everybody called Elizabeth Brown McGraw either Betty or Bets. A divorcée with two adorable girls, she was tall, stoic, and slightly bookish. "Regal" was the word my dad used whenever he showered her with compliments. And she, like Dad, was a saver. While many of the women Dad had dated yearned for fancy dinners or nights out on the town, Mom preferred simple things. Walks in the park. Trips to the library. Picnics with my half sisters, Cindy and Marguerite. All the better to save money toward buying and furnishing a nice house. She was a woman who spoke his language. Dad was smitten.

Life is full of little ironies. Even after their marriage fell apart, Mom and Dad seemed to get along better than many of the parents who chaperoned our events. They talked to us kids and to each other, while other parents stood side by side in the gym but appeared to be galaxies apart. In retrospect, the forces that had stifled my father's military career prepared him, in an odd way, for single parenthood. I'm not sure he would have been capable of running such a tight ship at home had he not spent much of his naval service in mess halls. Often the indignities and despair we endure can serve us in surprising ways. The U.S. military, while deserving of reproach for its treatment of men and women of color, has paradoxically become an institution that best models the concept of equal opportunity.

Here's another little irony: while Dad was the steadfast parent, keeping the ship afloat when Mom decamped, he was a mourned absence when I myself became a parent. He didn't live long enough to meet my husband or hold his grandchildren or listen to his daughter on the radio. Now it's my once absent mother who has become the mighty ballast for all of us: her siblings, my sister, my husband and I, her grandchildren, and the elderly ladies in her condominium, who always seek her wisdom and recipes.

Now I understand that she has always been there for me, even when her actions caused me pain and confusion. Like most black mothers in our neighborhood—indeed, all of America—Mom was hyperattentive about taming my long, thick, kinky hair. With the exception of Easter Sunday, she kept my hair in braids. When I was young, she tied a profusion of teeny ones. I would sleep with a little pink sponge roller hanging on my forehead to effect little sausage roll bangs, which would frizz like antennae the minute I stepped on the playground. It didn't matter that my bangs never lasted beyond lunchtime. When I got home, Mom would hit those tufts of hair with a dollop of DuSharme or VO5 and pull out the sponge roller to commence the process all over again.

When I was older, we set aside the rollers and the gum-ball hair ties and went for two long Pocahontas braids separated by a center part. As my hair got longer and seemingly thicker, with each passing year, Mom stopped washing it herself in the kitchen sink and sent me instead to various neighborhood "kitchen beauticians," women who could work magic with a hot comb and a hair dryer in the same space where they churned out fried chicken and coleslaw. Over time, some of these kitchen beauticians became proper businesswomen, like Miss Olivia and Miss Debbie, who got their husbands to turn their basement recreation rooms into full-service salons, with reclining shampoo chairs and upright dryers. After years of hearing me wince and cry as Mom worked her way through my tangles on Saturday night, Dad did not complain when my hairdresser visits were added to the family budget. The hairdressers would wash, dry, and straighten my hair and then quickly work it into a hairdo, always involving braids.

A few months after Mom left, she announced that she was taking me for a haircut. I assumed she meant a trim, because most of her hair-care advice revolved around helping my hair grow. "Eat your vegetables. . . . Here's a spoonful of cod liver oil. . . . Make sure to wrap your head up at night. . . . Don't wear a wool hat any longer than you have to. . . . Make sure to put curler paper over your sponge rollers so that congealed foam won't pull your hair out. . . . Don't play with your ends. . . . Wear a swim cap. . . . Forget about bobbing for apples at that birthday party just 'cause the other kids are doing it. . . . Use a boar-bristle brush. . . . Thank the Good Lord you have a healthy head of hair." I've always wondered whether there is some kind of encyclical spelling out the cardinal commands of black hair care, rules my mother followed to the letter.

That spring day, when we left our neighborhood and headed downtown, she had something else in mind. I thought maybe we were going to one of the "real" salons, where lawyers and newscasters got their hair and nails done. I soon realized that Mom had a different plan when we arrived at a barbershop. I'd spent enough time with my father at barbershops on the South Side of Minneapolis to know that women rarely entered these sanctums. If they did, they were usually, like me, accompanying a customer. Or they were young women who'd freed themselves from the tyranny of the hot comb to go natural with an Afro.

When Mom and I made our way into the downtown barbershop, I would soon be, unbeknownst to me, of the latter category. The barbershop was nothing like the place where Dad spent an hour every Saturday morning. It was in the IDS Tower, which at the time was the tallest building in the state. Even if you've never been to Minneapolis, you might recall the glass skyscraper, for in her weekly television sitcom Mary Tyler Moore would take the measure of it and toss her tam in the air. The barbershop was inside the building's cavernous lobby, and it was so much fancier than any place the men I knew went to get their hair cut. While a few barbers there wore the standard short-sleeved white coats, most were dressed like disco kings, in bell bottoms and shirts with wide collars. This, Mom explained, was where the truly cool came to get their Afros shaped and refined. Afros?

Mom said these barbers were great at creating the singular Afro best suited to the shape of a person's face and lifestyle. Her fingers flew through my hair as she worked the rubber bands out, uncoiled my braids, and shook out my waves. She guided me toward a burgundy pleather chair, where a barber stood attentively. "Michele," she said, "you're going to look so cute in a kinky little Afro."

Was I not supposed to have a say in this? Wasn't someone going to ask me if I wanted an Afro? I'd spent years growing my hair out so I could stand in the bathroom at night, undo my braids, and pretend I was Marilyn McCoo of the 5th Dimension or Ali McGraw or, for that matter, any of the long, straight-haired models who stared back at me from magazine covers. Now many of my style icons at the time wore Afros. I adored *Get Christie Love.* I was crazy about the Jackson 5. I pined for Michael Jackson, but I didn't want to look like him.

Mom tried to convince me that "the look" was right for me. She talked of how easy it would be to care for. As summer was just a few weeks away, she said, "Imagine being able to swim as much as you want without worrying about losing your press and curl. It just makes good sense." And when she noticed that pushing the practicality of the new do was not winning over a thirteen-year-old, she switched back to flattery: "You have such a pretty little face. A cute little Afro will really show it off."

Whether I'd have a say in the matter or not, I, more than likely, didn't want to rock the boat, as my outings with Mom, after she'd moved out, were sporadic. So I held my breath and tried not to cry as a barber sporting plaid pants, gold rings, and his own outsized Afro snipped inch after inch of my hair, from my elbows to my shoulders and past my ears, then going in for the kill: trimming the halo of fuzz that remained. I remember feeling slightly sick when I looked at the floor and saw all the hair I used to braid at night and toss over my shoulder or coil on my head. Mom in bell bottoms, standing at the doorway, didn't understand how painful this was for me.

Once the mounds of my hair had been swept away, Mom leaned in, put her face next to mine, and we both stared ahead at the mirror. "You look so cute!" she exclaimed, in a tone sincere enough to suggest a sales pitch. I remember thinking the Afro was, after all, kind of cute. But that was the problem: at thirteen I was done with cute. I wanted to be glamorous. I wanted to look like the models in magazines. I wanted to run out of the building and find Mary Tyler Moore's tam and pull it down tight over my head. "Looking good," the barber said. "Looking good, babygirl."

I've never liked the phrase "looking good." It sounds lustful, lascivious, praise as complimentary as a pat on the tush. No thanks. Mom could see I was about to cry and she whispered, "You do look good." The problem was, I didn't feel good. It had all happened too fast. I felt nauseous. Mom paid the disco barber, and we headed home. On the way to the car, Mom stopped to buy me an ice cream cone. My favorite, peppermint bon bon. When she wasn't looking, I threw it in a trash can.

I was so mad I walked a few feet behind her, even when she slowed down to let me catch up. I stared at the ground and, as was my habit at the time, chewed my bottom lip. When I looked up, I noticed something: black people, especially black women, were nodding approvingly at me in passing, as if to say, in today's parlance, "You go, girl!" This kept happening for weeks, even as my Afro got bigger and bigger, eventually growing so large that it reached past the frame of my school photos. Sometimes, when a be-Afroed woman would lean down at me and whisper, "Little sister, I like that 'fro," I'd smile. But the fact that I looked more like a boy than a girl was not lost on the playground, where the kids were unmerciful.

With the rise of Afrocentrism and black power in politics, music, and popular culture, my Afro had given me cachet long before I knew what the word meant. And it made life easier for Dad and me. He had no idea how to set, or braid, or smooth out hair that had a mind of its own. Afros, he understood. By the seventies, he had even let his own closely cropped hair grow an inch or two, and wore a slight goatee.

I've asked Mom a hundred times why she cut my hair that day; she's always breezy, ready with a pat answer: "It seemed like a good idea." Or "I thought you would look cute in a 'fro." But I think I know what she was doing: trying to do her part, while not living with Dad and me, to keep me from becoming that teenage ingenue I so badly wanted to be. She was not present consistently enough to offer guidance or to prevent boys from sniffing around. Or she may have been trying to make life easier for Dad regarding my hair-care regimen. Betty Norris was a mother looking out for her daughter's best interest. It took me years before I figured out as much, and years before I made peace with it.

Though I am loath to admit it, Mom may have been right about my hair, as she was about more important matters: for instance, that the shooting incident at the Pythian Temple and Dad's secrecy about it went a long way toward explaining many a curiosity in our family, including the simmering tension between Uncle Simpson and Dad. While my father remained close to his brothers in Chicago, a mild conflict would flare up between Belvin and Simpson at unexpected moments. I never understood why until I dug into my father's story. Simpson had planned to use his military stipend and back pay to buy property in Chicago or start his own business. But after Dad was arrested, my grandparents insisted that he use his nest egg to bail his brothers out of the Birmingham jail, pay for a lawyer, and dole out payola as needed to hasten his brothers' departure from a legal system that was byzantine at best when blacks were involved. The idea was to make the whole thing go away.

Simpson's son Butch said his dad quietly seethed every time he told the story about the squelching of his dream. Simpson often ribbed Dad about an outstanding loan. Though he appeared to speak in jest, there was always a caustic undertone to his remarks that even a kid could detect. My father would look more pained than amused. The squabble between the two loving brothers would surface when they spent too much time together. It reached a head once during a summer trip to Itasca State Park. Simpson and his wife, Ernestine, drove to Minneapolis to join my parents and me for a long trip north to Itasca, in the northern part of the state. I was about ten; my older sisters had long outgrown mandatory summer vacation with the parents, as had Simpson's two sons. So the two Norris couples and I embarked on our excellent adventure in Dad's white Galaxie 500 sedan.

Once at Itasca, I spent most of my time with my nose in a book, while the adults drank Scotch and sodas and played bid whist. After one singular late night of card playing and rambunctious laughter, Mom and Aunt Ernestine slept in, while Dad, Uncle Simpson, and I headed to the big dining hall in the Old Rustic Lodge to have an early breakfast. At some point that morning, the ribbing between the brothers intensified. Simpson relentlessly put salt in whatever wound there was until my dad stormed off, muttering under his breath, leaving behind a little black skillet filled with grilled trout and scrambled eggs. I'd rarely seen my father lose his temper. It unsettled me, but it tickled my uncle. Uncle Simpson invited me for a walk to the water, so that my father would have some time to shake off whatever was bothering him.

Itasca is a gorgeous spot. There, the mighty Mississippi begins its meandering twenty-five-hundred-mile journey toward the Gulf of Mexico. Massive pine trees hug the shoreline, and the sun lingers at the close of the day, long golden rays piercing the lacework of branches. But the dark side of sunrise is so chilly—even in summer—that thick mist rises from the water. That morning, I skipped my way across the Mississippi in the time it takes to spell the word. The river there is only about twenty feet wide. The Twin Cities, Minneapolis and Saint Paul, are separated by a yawn of roiling muck flowing beneath the massive bridges joining one town to the other. Up in Itasca State Park, you can walk back and forth, across big jagged rocks, from one shore of the Mississippi to the other. Uncle Simpson held my hand as we did this, he in his dress shoes, trying his best to keep up with me in my Keds.

Simpson used to call his sons "Rusty-butt boys" and held them in line by barking orders and taking no guff. He was, however, different around his nieces, slipping us peppermints and breaking out in applause when we sang silly songs or twirled until we fell. That morning, after we traversed the Mississippi, he leaned down to me and whispered, "You just crossed a river on your own two feet—now you can do anything."

I believed him with all my heart. And even though at the time I knew nothing about the events at the Pythian Temple, I must also somehow have believed the gist of his contention over money with Dad; their tart exchange that morning had a ring of truth because of its effect on my father. Dad spent his life making sure he didn't owe anybody anything. He paid his credit card bills in full, and racked up as much overtime as possible at the post office. He was so averse to debt that he sent in extra money with his mortgage payment every month to help chip away at the principal. But cash alone could not settle the ledger with Simpson. Simpson had spent money earned in America's fight for freedom to keep his brother out of jail, sacrificing his own dreams in the bargain. Short of that never having happened, it would be impossible for Belvin to repay his debt to his brother in full.

Once the Norris brothers left their hometown of Birmingham, most remained only lightly tethered to the city. Dad, however, was for the rest of his life fiercely loyal to his parents and to the city of his birth. He may have fled Alabama, but he didn't stay away. He visited more frequently than any of his brothers. It wasn't apparent to his family in Minnesota, but the past had a strong pull on my father. His almost yearly pilgrimages to Birmingham and his insistence on sending me down to visit my grandparents every summer are perplexing in light of what happened to him after the war. But I suppose that, as Faulkner said, he must have believed that "the past is never dead. It's not even past." For him the road ahead would always be much more rugged without the solace afforded by taking heed of where he'd been. Not only did Alabama pull him back; so did many checkpoints of his military career. San Francisco. New Orleans. Pensacola. Northern Virginia. Once I'd studied his military records, I realized that the better part of our family vacation destinations were places where he'd served. Not even my mom knew that, and I could tell she was unnerved when I revealed the fact.

Dad had wanderlust. He loved to travel. Denied a chance for higher education, he was always on the hunt for new learning experiences. On a postal worker's salary, he managed to set aside money for theater tickets, Book-of-the-Month Club selections, museum workshops, and a subscription to the Sunday *New York Times.* He was constantly telling us kids, "Learn all you can," and to show us he meant business, he led by example. He and my mother read constantly. Novels. Plays. Trade journals. Textbooks they purchased during the annual lost-books sale at the main post office. And most importantly, vacations. While we'd hit the typical tourist sights wherever we went, the highlight for him was wandering off the beaten path.

We'd head out in the morning with change jangling in Dad's pockets to board a city bus or trolley bound for ordinary vicinities. Dad would always say he wanted to see how average folk lived. He wanted to eat in the restaurants they ate in and visit the parks where they taught their kids how to hit baseballs. But I wonder now if he wasn't intent on visiting neighborhoods that had once been off-limits to black servicemen, much the way a child, denied ice cream, will gorge himself on it at the first possible chance. Perhaps he was retracing the steps of his early life out of mere nostalgia. Perhaps he needed to have the last word vis-à-vis his experiences of segregation. Perhaps he wanted to prove to those who'd stamped "Negro" on all his military records that the word alone did not encompass all he was or all he had to offer.

We always returned from vacation with uncanny stories. An especially peculiar one concerned the Vietnam War. While traveling through Winnepeg, Manitoba, Dad would spot grungy young black men with enormous backpacks. He knew by instinct that they were in Canada because they were draft dodgers, and he would go out of his way to chat them up. On more than one occasion he'd offer them a deal. He'd buy them dinner if they agreed to tell him why they chose to flee the United States rather than fight for their country overseas. At the time I thought his obsession was just one of his eccentricities. A sage trying to understand youthful impulsiveness. I had no idea that his "let me buy you a burger" altruism might have provided an opening into his hidden past. When he sat there quizzing those bedraggled fugitives, I rolled my eyes in pubescent perturbation.

In spite of his experiences in the military, my father was unwaveringly patriotic, which manifested itself in myriad little ways. He planted small flags throughout the yard on the Fourth of July. And during the summer parade season he would retrieve them from the hall closet so we could wave them from the side of the road as the floats and marching bands passed by. These were the very flags he pulled out one Sunday night, as he and I watched a TV special on the American bicentennial. It was 1976, and I was fourteen years old. Dad was in his fifties and all decked out in red, white, and blue, down to a pair of socks adorned with stars and stripes. He sat in his favorite armchair in front of our black-and-white TV (Dad refused to splurge on a color set) so he could watch a star-spangled affair that would culminate with stunning fireworks above the National Mall. He loved fireworks—even when transmitted in shades of gray by a nineteen-inch Magnavox.

At the time, the prospect of sitting with my father while indulging in corny jingoism, as it seemed to me, was horrifying. But Dad's enthusiasm was contagious. In truth, so, too, was the pull of his loneliness. I found myself declining invitations to go on dates or hang out at the 7-Eleven with my friends, so that I could be with him to watch TV or play bid whist. Sometimes we'd go hit golf balls after dinner, then stop by the Dairy Queen. It would have been a little too pitiful to imagine him, in front of the TV, waving his miniature star-spangled banner by himself to celebrate the bicentennial. We wound up in the living room, waving silly flags and eating peanuts from the shell—something Mom would never have allowed. The marginalized veteran, in his own way, insisted, "I, too, sing America."

In celebrating America—or, as he called it, "the U.S. of A."—Belvin Norris collected stamps and spent sixteen dollars every pay period to purchase a new coin from the Franklin Mint History of the United States series, until he amassed the entire set. He took great pride in his work at the post office, and in the fact that he worked for the federal government. While he may have hidden his World War II medal in the back of a bureau drawer and forgotten it, he lovingly arranged, in the little wooden valet in its top drawer, his twentieth- and thirtieth-anniversary postal service pins and his Mr. Zip tie clasps.

My father never sought wealth, fame, or power. Well, maybe he wouldn't have minded more money. His goal in life, instead, was to be the Average Joe of the American dream. He aspired to be ordinary. His brass ring was a solid middle-class life. And his pride was the house on Oakland Avenue and watching his family do all those little things that were beyond his reach when he was a young man. Now when I look at pictures of him I see a "we can do this too" twinkle in his eyes. He pushed us toward those things that were especially prized by white society. Perhaps it's why I wound up taking art history lessons at age ten, learning gymnastics on ice (and, as a result, earning a spot on the hockey cheerleading squad), and attending the University of Minnesota on weekends, while still in high school, for courses in science and engineering. Dad was my guiding star.

Having achieved working-class comfort, my parents always sought black middle-class affirmation in the neighborhood, on the news, and in popular culture. Seated on the matching sofa and love seat in our living room, in our integrated neighborhood in South Minneapolis, we would every week watch a television show called *Julia*. It debuted in 1968 featuring Diahann Carroll, the first African American actress to star in her own network sitcom. She played a hardworking Vietnam War widow who slept on a sofa so her little boy, Corey, could have his own bed. Julia was a nurse. She was beautiful and stylish and funny. She worked for a wise and crotchety old doctor played by Lloyd Nolan, and she had a way of standing up to her critics without getting their goat—a skill that many black Americans were trying to master themselves as they edged into an integrated society.

Julia was a crossover hit, eagerly watched by black and white families alike. My parents laughed at the jokes that went right over my head, delighted to see a show using comedy to tackle salient issues of the day. For my part, I focused on the weekly storyline concerning Julia's young son, Corey, and his white best friend, Earl J. Waggedorn. I was over the moon when I discovered a Julia Barbie doll under the Christmas tree and, for weeks, dragged it everywhere I went.

As much as we enjoyed *Julia*'s three-season run, my mother wondered, "Why can't she have a husband? How hard is that? It can't be about the salary, because she has boyfriends who take her out on dates almost every week, so they are paying someone. Why can't there be a man in the house?" At the time I thought Mom was being unduly harsh. Years later, when I interviewed Diahann Carroll, I discovered that she, too, had wanted to have a TV husband, but, for whatever reason, NBC and the show's creators were of a different mind. Hit though it was, the show was lambasted by some critics. *The Saturday Review,* for instance, claimed that the show was lacking in verisimilitude, opining that it was a "far, far cry from the bitter realities of Negro life in the urban ghetto."[1]

Who said all Negroes lived in the ghetto? We didn't! "The question that kept coming up at the time was, 'What kind of single black mother was I supposed to be as Julia anyway?' " Diahann Carroll wrote in her recent memoir. "Twentieth Century Fox and NBC expected the kind that got top Nielsen ratings! And yet the pressure to be someone else never let up in my three years on the show. . . . I was under the political microscope for Julia like you wouldn't believe. But I did not have the expertise to discuss the socioeconomic situation of the African-American community. Nor did I feel I should have to defend the character of a polite nurse with excellent taste in clothes, some of which I brought to the set from my own closet. I was simply trying to get comfortable playing a hardworking, financially strapped single mother who slept on a living-room sofa in a one-bedroom apartment."[2]

It would be several years after *Julia*'s last episode before black upper-middle-class life was portrayed on network television: first in *The Jeffersons,* about a family who struck it rich in their dry-cleaning business and moved on up to New York's East Side to a "dee-luxe" apartment in the sky. The show ran for eleven seasons, starting in 1975. Then, there was *The Cosby Show,* which ran from 1984 to 1992 and featured a blissfully happy family. Mom was a lawyer, Dad was a doctor, and the grandparents were proud graduates of historically black colleges.

Unlike on *The Jeffersons,* race was rarely overtly mentioned on *The Cosby Show;* nor was it necessary, for almost all of the show's story lines were inspirational, championing values embraceable by any race, culture, or nationality. This was its subversiveness at the time. Nowadays *The Cosby Show* is credited with tearing down barriers and creating opportunities for new shows featuring black casts and story lines. Upon the inauguration of Barack Obama, which happened to occur only a few months before the twenty-fifth anniversary of the start of the show, it was perhaps inevitable that pundits and critics would hyperventilate about how the Huxtables had somehow paved the way for the country to elect its first African American president. "When *The Cosby Show* was on, that was America's family," Karl Rove was quoted as saying after the election. "It wasn't a black family. It was America's Family."[3] I'm afraid it *was* a black family, one adored by America. Yet, more than a quarter century after the inception of the show, there are few, if any, families like the Huxtables on TV or movie screens.

My husband, Broderick Johnson, and I honeymooned in Italy, where we noticed something odd about the greetings we got everywhere we went. People kept calling us "the Robinsons." The restaurateur, the woman serving gelato, the police officer in the town square, the bank manager who looked vaguely like Omar Sharif—all bubbled with hospitality as if they'd known us, welcoming us, to our puzzlement, as "the Robinsons." "*Abbiamo sentito che si trovavano in zona.* ["We heard you were in the area."] *Benvenuti! Benvenuti,*" the storekeeper would yell, telling passersby to come meet the Robinsons!

We were staying along the shores of Lago d'Iseo, a picturesque lake in Lombardy. The mystery was solved near the end of our visit, at the home of our friends Rosa and Bepe. On their coffee table was a television guide, with Bill Cosby and Phylicia Rashad smiling on the cover under the headline "I Robinsons," Italian for "The Robinsons." We apparently reminded the Italians of Cosby and Rashad. But why were the Huxtables no longer the Huxtables? When I returned to the States, I got the answer from friends who worked for NBC. I learned that Huxtable had been changed to Robinson because Italians find the latter much easier to pronounce. But why Robinson? The surname was apparently associated with black success, thanks to Jackie Robinson's groundbreaking baseball career.

The whirligig of black success can be a curious thing. Saturdays are usually movie night at our house. My husband and I, our two kids, and various guests usually gather after dinner in the Red Room, a small den with lipstick-colored walls and bulky seating. After the long haul of the week, we spread out and munch popcorn and salty snacks while watching the DVD of the week—always a subject of protracted and self-interested give-and-take, as in any other American family. But I'm not sure that the conversation in our little red room one Saturday night was the sort that takes place in most American households—certainly not among white families.

Three generations had gathered for movie night that Saturday: my husband and I, our kids, their godfather James, and my first cousin's daughter Sophia, a college freshman. We were watching *Freedom Writers,* a feel-good drama about a white teacher trying to reform a classroom of minority kids caught up in southern California's gang life. The students have no appreciation for the school system, no use for education, and so no interest in reading, much less writing poetry. Yet their instructor, played by Hilary Swank (the story is based on the real experiences of a woman named Erin Gruwell), teaches them to respect themselves and each other. A savior in the hood, as it were. At one point, Erin Gruwell tries to order copies of *The Diary of Anne Frank* for the class, but a pert, blond administrator denies her request. The kids, the blonde says, are not worth the expense.

If you were sitting with us in the Red Room that night, you would have heard a collective gasp. Sophia, the college freshman, blurted out, "They have such low expectations for those kids, and they haven't even bothered to find out what they can do." Sophia's outburst surprised me. She's usually quiet, the only one among us with exquisite movie-watching etiquette. "My guidance counselor told me I should go to community college," she went on. "Didn't even try to get me to apply to four-year schools. She told me a four-year college would be too much pressure. I mean, can you believe that?"

"Believe? Oh, yeah," James shot back. "Teachers told me to forget about college and forget about trying to be a professional." James, it should be noted, is a Stanford graduate and a former pro football player. "No question. I know something about low expectations!" James was getting worked up. He jumped to his feet, waving a finger as he headed toward the fridge for some ice cream. "They said I was not Stanford material, and when I asked them why, they couldn't give me an answer. Not any kind of answer that made sense. It basically came down to: 'Kids like you can't really deal with that kind of pressure. Do yourself a favor and set your bar a bit lower.' "

Agog, I shook my head in disbelief, an appalled grin on my face. I, too, had been counseled to apply only to junior colleges, even though I'd set my sights on some prestigious institutions. I told the group my story, and Sophia, James, and I shared a shock of recognition. Each of us had assumed that if you were black, this kind of bias was just the deal. There was no need to dwell on it. James, I, and Sophia graduated from high school in 1969, 1979, and 2008, respectively, in different American cities. Three white guidance counselors, spanning nearly forty years after the beginning of integration and the rise of the civil rights movement, had willy-nilly tried—unsuccessfully, it must be said—to stymie the ambition of three black high school students. For that their motives should be questioned, if not denounced. But here we were swapping race war stories with righteous indignation. How many other black youths had been told to check their aspirations? Had they been damaged by the advice? Did they rise or fall as a result?

Both Dad and Mom would have scoffed at our conversation that Saturday night: Dad, who never spoke to his family about the humiliation of his shooting and the terrifying night he'd spent in a Birmingham jail upon returning as a World War II veteran; Mom, who'd kept her mother's turn as an itinerant Aunt Jemima a secret from her children, perhaps out of shame. Why? So as not to allow us to be hindered by acrimony and rancor in our struggle to rise above "the slings and arrows of outrageous fortune" and achieve self-fulfillment no matter what. How would I have been different without their complex grace of silence? And what's been more corrosive to the dialogue on race in America over the last half century or so, things said or unsaid? What racial legacy should Broderick and I bequeath to our children?

All the talk of a postracial America betrays an all too glib eagerness to put in remission a four-hundred-year-old cancerous social disease. We can't let it rest until we attend to its symptoms in ourselves and others. Jimmy Carter talking about white voter discomfiture with Barack Obama's race; Eric Holder suggesting that Americans are more often than not cowards in their refusal to address the subject candidly; Harry Reid surmising that Obama's advantages are his skin tone and lack of a "Negro" dialect: all have been subject to immediate and loud public censure by people more interested in excoriating them for daring to bring up the subject of race than willing to examine whether their statements bore hard truths.

So often the mere mention of the word *race* can make some people apoplectic or pious or frozen by anxiety, only to beat a hasty retreat to their comfort zone: grim taciturnity. Our collective discomfort with the issue is why discussions about race can so easily become so explosive. But our sensitivity renders us vulnerable to those who would exploit race for their own agenda, if not their ratings. Public discussions of race are very often a blood sport. Private conversations—with no audience, fewer sanctions, and, often, fewer filters—can be altogether another matter. They are no less painful—the hurt can be profound—but the results are almost always far more productive.

In the course of writing this book I've had conversations that made me weep and that made me want to holler from frustration. Many of the people I spoke with said disturbing things but had the courage to reassess themselves through the prism of their conflicting emotions. I hope you will appreciate their honesty, learn something from the bravery of their candor. When Julia Beaton spoke of her disdain for white people, she came to realize that that was not exactly what she meant, even as she heard herself speak. When Aubrey Justice said he didn't think he'd benefited from white privilege, he was presented with the opportunity to reexamine his life vis-à-vis that of others.

Our continuing national conversation on race will no doubt proceed by fits and starts and occasional spats and squabbles. But all of us should be willing to remain at the table even when things get uncomfortable. We need to be fearless while unburdening ourselves, even as we respect the same effort in others. There is often grace in silence. But there is always power in understanding.

On a trip to New York City I took my kids to the Intrepid Sea, Air and Space Museum, the centerpiece of which is a massive aircraft carrier now permanently docked in the Hudson River. We were out sightseeing for a couple of hours before taking the train back to D.C. I'd originally planned just to drive past the ship and point it out to them. But something told me we should make a proper visit. A battleship is much like a floating town, and I thought the kids would love to investigate its secret world. The *Intrepid* is a magnet for navy veterans and their families. That day I must have seen a dozen men wearing headgear, jackets, or sweatshirts announcing their service to their country. Military men often carry themselves a certain way; these senior citizens were erect and slightly stiff, with puffed-out chests. I've struggled to find the right words to describe the emotions that washed over me. My father was so present at that moment. Of course, he'd never served on the *Intrepid,* but he'd spent time aboard a navy ship.

At the entrance to the museum, we were greeted by a volunteer worker, an old gentleman wearing a yellow fleece *Intrepid* jacket, who ushered us toward an eight-minute film about the carrier. It showed us the *Intrepid*'s history, from World War II to Vietnam and on to 9/11—when the ship served as living quarters for the FBI. But, I soon discovered, the film presented only four shots of African Americans, and if you blinked, you might have missed them altogether. As we stepped out of the theater we again saw the man in the yellow fleece jacket. He suggested that we might want to head upstairs to see the main attractions: the hangar and flight decks.

"Where can we find the kitchen?" I asked.

"Excuse me, ma'am?"

"Where would we find the place where all the food for the sailors was prepared?"

"Down that way, past those two big signs, and down two flights," he said. "But I must tell you, this is a big ship and if you had to skip anything, I would say you could skip the mess area."

Undaunted, I pressed on: "I'd like to find the mess area. My father was in the navy, and that's where he spent most of his time. I want my children to see it." An awkward silence ensued. The man slowly began to turn red, a look of embarrassment washing over his face. He stammered a bit before he found his words. "Oh yes, of course." Then he sputtered, "Well, as I said, it's past those two signs and down the hall." I could feel him staring after us as we headed toward the stairs.

To be sure, we visited the hangar deck and the ready room, where pilots reviewed footage of their fighter plane runs. We also saw the cramped quarters of the specialists who tracked the enemy on radar and sat slumped over telegraph machines, transmitting secret codes to Washington. And, of course, we made our way to the big attraction, the flight deck, now outfitted with retired flying machines. We posed for pictures and ogled the sleek lines and sheer awesomeness of the airplanes. Eagles at rest. Still majestic. Still powerful. Quite beautiful. But the kids grew bored and were made antsy by winds whipping across the deck.

You see, my two young children were already exhausted from the thrill, the sheer joy of gawking at the *Intrepid*'s kitchen belowdecks, with its huge soup cauldrons and "ginormous" ovens. They had peeked into the tiny quarters where messmen used to sleep on triple-decker bunks that were suspended on chains hanging from the ceiling. These, for them, had been the highlights of the visit. It was all they talked about on the way to the train station.

Somewhere, Belvin Norris Jr. was smiling.

Epilogue

I WAS UNABLE TO SPEAK at my father's funeral. I was wrung out. Stunned and crazy with grief, I sat in the front pew clutching the Father's Day card I would have given him in the hospital if he'd held on one more day, instead of slipping away as Saturday yielded to the Sabbath. Everyone expected me—the journalist, the former cheerleader, the extrovert, the biological daughter—to get up and say something. A eulogy. A tribute or remembrance. I couldn't do it. I was twenty-six years old but made completely infantile by sorrow. Instead Uncle Joe rose and walked toward the little podium surrounded by a sunburst of gladiolus (a ridiculous name for showy flowers that are most often present in moments of grief).

"Good night, sweet prince." Joe Norris stood with one hand on his brother's casket. He quoted Shakespeare and Flaubert and made us chuckle with words written by Langston Hughes. He covered for me beautifully. All these years later, perhaps I have finally found the words to lift my father up as he deserved. I've come to realize that I may have been pinned to the pew because, deep down, I didn't really understand who he was.

How well do you know the people who raised you? Look around your dining room table. Look around at your loved ones, especially the elders. The grandparents and the aunts and uncles who used to give you shiny new quarters and unvarnished advice. How much do you really know about their lives? Perhaps you've heard that they served in a war, or lived for a time in a log cabin, or arrived in this country speaking little or no English. Maybe they survived the Holocaust or the Dust Bowl. How were they shaped by the Depression or the Cold War, or the stutter-step march toward integration in their own community? What were they like before they married or took on mortgages and assumed all the worries that attend the feeding, clothing, and education of their children? If you don't already know the answers, the people who raised you will most likely remain a mystery, unless you take the bold step and say: Tell me more about yourself.

Few of us actually believe that David slew the giant Goliath with nothing but a slingshot, or that a little Dutch boy prevented a massive flood by sticking his finger in a dike. These stories are allegories. So are many accounts we read in history books. History is made in lots of little ways every single day. We all know about the four young men who started a lunch-counter revolt by refusing to budge at a Greensboro Woolworth's. They weren't the only ones who stood up against restaurant segregation. They simply captured the attention of the *New York Times* and the television networks, and so their story was enshrined and is singularly presented in history books. But have you ever heard of Claudette Colvin? Susie McDonald? Aurelia Browder? How about Mary Louise Smith? Though I'm sure you've heard of Rosa Parks.

Rosa Parks was, of course, the woman who amplified the news of the civil rights movement by quietly saying no when asked to get up and move out of the whites-only section of a city bus. But long before Rosa Parks and her legendary act of defiance, other black women also shook their heads and said no, standing up against segregated public transportation. Claudette Colvin. Susie McDonald. Aurelia Browder. Mary Louise Smith.

Maybe their families know the role they played. Maybe not. And if they did, maybe they stopped talking about it, so painful was it to recall a relative being unjustly and forcibly led off a bus in handcuffs. Maybe they didn't want to poison the minds of the family's youth by dwelling on segregation and racial hatred. Maybe, while waxing nostalgic, they mistook the fidgetiness of a young one as impatience with or repudiation of their yesteryear experiences. Perhaps these old men and women now sit at lace-covered tables every holiday, surrounded by grandchildren, nieces, and nephews who have no idea that the dainty little old woman mashing up her peas put a down payment on their futures five decades before by confronting segregation codes.

Many steps lead to the crossing of a threshold, and many are the people, often anonymous, who play minor roles in history's grand tales. I am betting that some of them might be sitting at your family table. They might take their tales to their graves if you don't invite them to share their stories and wisdom. But "Tell me more about yourself" will likely be just a start. You'll never learn much at just one sitting. Be persistent: string together some simple questions, then sit back, shut up, and listen.

You'll find out amazing things about your family, and thereby learn essential things about yourself. Be patient. Be gentle. Record the stories if you can. Invite the children to participate; get them to ask questions, because their natural curiosity has not yet been tinged by judgment. And remember, food always helps. A piece of pie. A slab of pound cake. A nice square of noodle kugel. Something delicious to enliven the senses and stir the memory. The atmosphere should say, "I am here with you; I'm listening." There is grace in silence, and power to be had from listening to that which, more often than not, was left unsaid.

ACKNOWLEDGMENTS

I could not have written this book without the support of my family. My husband, Broderick Johnson, reminds me every day that Love is the best part of any story. Always & Forever are more than just words. You are my heart. For Aja, Norris, and Broddy, I hope this book helps you understand Grace in all its many forms. At our dinner table you learn that Grace is that thing that must be said before a meal. In school, you learn that dictionaries define Grace as a disposition to kindness and compassion. In life, I hope you learn that Grace is also measured by how you climb up the rough side of a mountain and what you do with your life once you get there.

I am forever grateful to my agent and dear friend Gail Ross, who believed that I had a story to tell, and used her mighty "mama bear" skills to nudge me toward this path. I must have won the lottery when my editor, Erroll McDonald, signed on to this project. You understood the power in this story and provided a careful eye, a hungry ear, a depth of knowledge, and a playful sense of humor just when it was needed most. (DuSharme!) Thank you for your patience and supreme confidence as this project transformed into something neither of us imagined when we set out on this journey.

I enjoyed the warm embrace of enthusiasm for this project early on at Pantheon. Katie Freeman and Paul Bogaards marshaled a team that worked hard to make sure this book found a home on many a bookshelf. Lily Evans is as gracious as her name suggests and such a joy to work with.

I have long believed that you learn much of what you need to get through life at the dining room table in your childhood home. In that sense my parents and grandparents were tremendous tutors for they taught me the most important lessons about surviving life's storms, making your own luck, and making the most with what you've got if luck is in short supply. From the moment I entered this world, my oldest sister, Marguerite, shared her love of books with me, and though she no longer lives on this earth, she was with me every step of this journey. My sister Cindy is a divine source of inspiration who lifts our entire family up with her wise guidance, dedication to others, and incredible vigor. Superwoman could learn a thing or two from you. I certainly have. Thanks for always telling me I'm capable of anything. It would be so easy to throw "almost" into that sentence. You never do. I hope this book will serve as a tribute in at least some small way to the folks who know me as "Mickey," that protective cocoon of aunts, uncles, cousins, and loving neighbors who occupied my world in Minneapolis, Chicago, and Birmingham. Mary and Luther Johnson and the rest of the Johnson clan were abundantly generous with their time and support. I hope the next generation, Carlos, Carniesha, and Moon, find strength in these pages. I hope this book honors the memory of William Johnson, who like my father, served his country well in the years before the navy fully integrated. Myrtle Brotherton and Mimi Worku are heaven-sent members of our family circle. Thank you for all the many things you do to nourish our home, body, and soul.

There is the family that you're born unto, the family you marry into, and then there are the family members you adopt along the way. This book proved my village is a thing of awe. My sister-friend Gwen Ifill has been my best pal since the day decades ago when she hijacked my rental car for a Texas shopping spree. Thank you for being my bedrock during every step of this process. I cherish your friendship. Richard Wollfe and Paula Cuello Wolffe provided strong shoulders, delicious food, and valuable wisdom. You are trusted confidants, dedicated parents, and adopted members of our extended family tree.

James Ferguson and Marcia Jones-Ferguson were always there with love, laughter, and guiding hands for our young kids. Sharon Malone and The Honorable Eric Holder helped me understand that our children deserve our time but they *need* our history. Cheryl and Eric Whitaker reminded me that simple stories have great power at the moment when this project took a sharp left turn. Jim Halpert, Karen Kornbluh, Marilyn Milloy, Arvyce Walton, Christie Worrell, Maggie Michael, Dwight Bush and Toni Cook-Bush, William and Michelle Jawando, and Andy and Glay Blocker must have special powers because you all knew when I needed a word of encouragement and swooped in at just the right moment. Once I found the truth, Robert Raben helped me understand it.

From start to finish, I was buoyed by a fabulous team of researchers, first readers, and guides. Jim Baggett runs the Department of Archives and Manuscripts at the Birmingham Public Library, and I suspect you might find wings if you look under his well-pressed shirts. He is truly an Angel. Karl Evanzz is the best researcher a writer could ask for. He deserves his own superhero cape for his dogged work and his lovely way with language. I can't wait to read *your* books. I have long been impressed with Marilyn Thompson's writing, research, and editing skills, which she put to great use in guiding me as I wrestled this story to the ground. Pamela Jones taught me much about Birmingham history *and* clingstone peaches. Jessica Alpert helped get this project off the ground, and Chris Benderev helped me get to the finish line. Deb Reeb transformed hours of tape into documents I could devour. Thanks to Janna Worsham in Senator Christopher Bond's office for helping me navigate the military personnel records center in Missouri. The Douglas County Historical Society in Minnesota was amazingly helpful, particularly Verne Weiss.

Thanks also to the long list of researchers and guides who provided their expertise, including Brian Nosek, Maurice Manring, Marilyn Kern-Foxworth, Ken Smikle, Catherine Fosl, Margaret Burnham, Horace Huntley and the staff of the Birmingham Civil Rights Institute, Kristen Pauker, Tony Greewald, Mahzarin Benaji, Radhika Parameswaran, Alvin Pouissant, Henry Louis Gates, Thomas Guglielmo, Jennifer Richeson, Tiffany Johnson at the Alabama State FOP, Ruben Davis, James Armstrong, the Alumni of A. H. Parker High School, Joe Picharillo, Douglas Blackmon, Deborah Willis, and Michael Eric Dyson.

Thoreau had his cabin in the woods. I had Tom Wetherell's special place on Martha's Vineyard.

Chris Nelson and Andrea Hsu helped me tackle the technical requirements for taping and storing interviews in all kinds of complicated situations. Melissa Gray and Dorie Greenspan helped me understand the power of food to coax delicious conversations. Ellen Silva twice gave this a loving once-over.

Everyone needs friends like Susan Feeney and Madhulika Sikka in their world. Mine is an immeasurably better place thanks to them.

I am indebted to NPR and the staff of *All Things Considered* for the tolerance that allowed me to work on this project while juggling the demands of a daily two-hour news program. There simply are not enough Fridays or enough pizzas or adequate words to say THANK YOU. Working with you is an honor and a heck of a lot of fun. I love you all. Special thanks to Robert Siegel and Melissa Block, Rhonda Ray, and in particular to our executive producer, Chris Turpin. You did not hit the ceiling (at least not in my presence) when I asked for "a bit more time to finish," and you offered your unending support for a project that created many complications for our staff. Thanks for letting me frolic temporarily in a different playground. Most of all, thanks for believing in me. Ellen Weiss has taken NPR to new heights, and she is not close to being done yet.

I should have known my partner in radio, Steve Inskeep, was up to something when he started asking me a series of questions about my past. Those conversations helped kick-start this project and cement what I hope is a lifelong allegiance. The residents of York, Pennsylvania, who demonstrated enormous courage when they accepted our invitation to sit down and talk about race, gave me the guts to look over my shoulder and delve headlong into family history.

To the members of St. Augustine Catholic Church in Washington, thank you for providing the guiding light that ever burns bright. And I am grateful for all those Maret parents and teachers who through their love and friendship provide the community quilt that shelters my children when duty calls. Hugs to my circle of sister girls, Gwen, Lisa, Sharon, Sheryll, Cheryl, Ertharin, Susan, Ann, Athelia, A'Lelia, Arjelia, Dez, Toni, SuSu, Marilyn, Amy, Kathy, Tia, Gena, Lynne, Donna, Michelle and the Cassandras. Enchanté! Heartfelt appreciation to all those, too many in number to name here, who are there for me when I am standing in the need of prayer, laughter, advice, a soothing hand, or something good to eat.

For Daddy,
your grace has been my best guide in life.

Finally to my Mother,
you are my North Star.

NOTES

3 *Aunt Jemimas*

1. "Only Negro Alexandria High Graduate Portrays Version of 'Aunt Jemima,' " *Park Region Echo* (Alexandria, Minn.), October 3, 1950.
2. M. M. Manring, *Slave in a Box: The Strange Career of Aunt Jemima* (Charlottesville: University of Virginia Press, 1998), p. 112.
3. Ibid., p. 118.
4. Judy Foster Davis, "*Aunt Jemima Is Alive and Cookin': An Advertiser's Dilemma of Competing* Collective Memories" (Paper presented at the Conference on Historical Analysis and Research in Marketing: The Future of Marketing's Past, 2005).

8 *Service*

1. *"Kolombangara and Vella Lavella 6 August–7 October 1943," United States Navy Combat Narrative* (Washington, D.C.: Naval Historical Center, Department of the Navy), pp. 1–8.
2. *The Negro in the Navy in World War II,* United States Naval Administrative Histories of World War II (Washington, D.C.: Naval Historical Section, Department of the Navy, n.d.), p. 14.
3. Ibid., p. 11.
4. Ibid., p. 9.
5. "Army & Navy: Black Sailors," *Time,* August 17, 1942.
6. *Guide to Command of Negro Naval Personnel* (Washington, D.C.: Navy Department, Bureau of Naval Personnel, February 12, 1945).
7. *The Negro in the Navy in World War II,* p. 50
8. Phillip McGuire, ed., *Taps for a Jim Crow Army: Letters from Black Soldiers in World War II* (Lexington: University Press of Kentucky, 1993), p. 28.
9. Lucille B. Milner, "A New Negro Will Return from the War: February 1944," *New Republic,* March 13, 1944.

9 *The Shooting*

1. Catherine Fosl, *Subversive Southerner: Anne Braden and the Struggle for Racial Justice in the Cold War South* (Lexington: University Press of Kentucky, 2006), p. 73.
2. Anne Braden, *The Wall Between* (New York: Monthly Review Press, 1958), p. 24.

3. Alabama Humanities Foundation and Auburn University, "World War II and Alabama," The Encyclopedia of Alabama (September 2007), at www.encyclopediaofalabama.org.

10 *The War at Home*

1. Steven F. Lawson, *Black Ballots: Voting Rights in the South, 1944–1969* (Lanham, Md.: Lexington Books, 1999), pp. 59–94.
2. "Birmingham War Vets March Through Streets for Vote Rights," *Chicago Defender* (national edition), February 2, 1946.
3. Lawson, p. 92; and V. O. Key Jr., *Southern Politics: In State and Nation* (New York: Alfred A. Knopf, 1949), pp. 646–63.
4. Letter from Eugene (Bull) Connor to President Franklin D. Roosevelt, August 7, 1946, Holdings of the Franklin D. Roosevelt Library.
5. John Egerton, *Speak Now Against the Day: The Generation Before the Civil Rights Movement in the South* (Chapel Hill: University of North Carolina Press, 1994), p. 362; Robin D. G. Kelley, *Race Rebels: Culture, Politics and the Black Working Class* (New York: Free Press, 1994), pp. 51, 64–65; and Nell Irvin Painter, *Creating Black Americans: African-American History and Its Meanings, 1619 to the Present* (New York: Oxford University Press, 2006), p. 232.
6. Anne Braden, *The Wall Between* (New York: Monthly Review Press, 1958), p. 29.
7. Oral History Interview with Modjeska Simkins, July 28, 1976, Southern Oral History Program Collection.
8. "Flogging Laid to Klan Group," *Sarasota Herald-Tribune,* June 6, 1946; and "Klan Flogged Negro Navy Veteran Near Atlanta, Says Arnall Aide," *Miami News,* June 7, 1946.
9. Committee Against Jim Crow in Military Service and Training, memo to Legal Committee, American Veterans Committee, October 30, 1947.
10. Martha Biondi, *To Stand and Fight: The Struggle for Civil Rights in Postwar New York City* (Cambridge: Harvard University Press, 2006), p. 47.
11. Michael J. Klarman, *From Jim Crow to Civil Rights: The Supreme Court and the Struggle for Racial Equality* (New York: Oxford University Press, 2004), p. 274; Manning Marable, *Race, Reform, and Rebellion: The Second Reconstruction and Beyond in Black America, 1945–2006* (Jackson: University Press of Mississippi, 2007), p. 25; Patricia Sullivan, *Lift Every Voice: The NAACP and the Making of the Civil Rights Movement* (New York: New Press, 2009), p. 317; and Harry S. Ashmore, *Civil Rights and Wrongs: A Memoir of Race and Politics, 1944–1996* (Columbia: University of South Carolina Press, 1997), p. 58.
12. Laura Wexler, *Fire in a Canebrake: The Last Mass Lynching in America* (New York: Scribner, 2003), pp. 57–69.
13. Andrew Myers, "The Blinding of Isaac Woodard," *The Proceedings of the South Carolina Historical Association* (Columbia, S.C.: South Carolina Department of Archives and History, 2004); and Andrew Myers, "Resonant Ripples in a Global Pond: The Blinding of Isaac Woodard," *Isaac Woodard,* Sworn Testimony for Civil Lawsuit, November 1947 (NAACP Papers, Reel 30, Frames 121–33). Also newspaper citations from the *Aiken Standard and Review,* the *Charleston Daily Mail,* the *State* (Columbia, S.C.), the *New York Times,* the *New York Amsterdam News,* the *Charleston Gazette* (West Virginia), and the *Landmark* (Statesville, N.C.).

14. Isaac Woodard Affidavit, April 1946 (NAACP Papers, Reel 28, Frames 1012–13).
15. Isaac Woodard Statement to FBI, September 1946 (NAACP Papers, Reel 28, Frame 911).
16. "Doomed Man Offers Eyes to Blind Vet," *Pittsburgh Courier,* December 14, 1946.
17. Ibid.
18. Orson Welles Radio Commentaries, including "Affidavit of Isaac Woodard," "The Place Was Batesburg," "Welles Film Banned," "To Be Born Free," and "The Peacemakers."
19. Michael R. Gardner, *Harry Truman and Civil Rights: Moral Courage and Political Risks* (Carbondale: Southern Illinois University Press, 2002), p. 131.
20. Letter from Harry Truman to Ernest W. Roberts, August 18, 1948, cited in Robert H. Feffell, *Off the Record: The Private Papers of Harry S. Truman* (New York: Harper & Row, 1980), pp. 146–47.
21. Quoted in Gardner, p. 47.

11 *A Date with Justice*

1. *Report of Citizen's Committee on Birmingham Police Department,* February 19, 1952, Department of Southern History and Literature, Birmingham Public Library, Birmingham, Alabama.

12 *Home*

1. The criticism appeared in an article written by television critic Robert Lewis Shayon in the *Saturday Review* May 1968, quoted in David R. Farber and Beth L. Bailey, *The Columbia Guide to America in the 1960s* (New York: Columbia University Press, 2003), p. 400.
2. Diahann Carroll, *The Legs Are the Last to Go: Acting, Marrying & Other Things I Learned the Hard Way* (New York: Amistad, 2008), p. 131.
3. Tim Arango, "Before Obama, There Was Bill Cosby," *New York Times,* November 8, 2008.

About the Author

Michele Norris, cohost of NPR's *All Things Considered,* was chosen as Journalist of the Year in 2009 by the National Association of Black Journalists and is cowinner of an Alfred I. duPont-Columbia University Award for *The York Project: Race and the '08 Vote.* She has appeared on *Meet the Press, Charlie Rose,* and the *Chris Matthews Show,* and has written for, among other publications, *The Washington Post,* the *Chicago Tribune,* and the *Los Angeles Times.* Washington, D.C., is the city she now calls home. She is married to Broderick Johnson and has two children, Aja and Norris, and a stepson, Broderick Jr.